THE SLIDING ZONE DEFENSE
FOR WINNING BASKETBALL

THE SLIDING ZONE DEFENSE
FOR WINNING BASKETBALL

JOHN S. EGLI

PARKER PUBLISHING COMPANY, INC.
West Nyack, N.Y.

PRINTED IN THE UNITED STATES OF AMERICA

13-813071-x   BC

DEDICATION

To the founder of this defense, Dr. John D. Lawther, my college coach; Colonel Luther R. Barth, my high school coach; the young men who played for me; the members of the coaching profession; to my wife, Nathel, and three children, Bonnie, Joe and Carol; and to my mother, who is our greatest defender, I dedicate this book.

What This Book Will Do for You

This book reveals a different concept of basketball which will enhance the success of any high school or college basketball team. The Sliding Zone Defense has been a key factor in our success at Penn State for 32 years, and it can also bring success to you.

The book explains why the Sliding Zone Defense (known by many as the "Penn State Sliding Zone"), and its variations are most effective for use in high school and collegiate competition. Included are the drills found most useful for developing the skills essential to a zone defense as well as the adaptations of the basic Sliding Zone strategy used to combat the many different types of offense.

A team can incorporate the basic slides into the "two out–three back," the "three out–two back," the "two-one-two," the full- or half-court press, and many other formations. These will be explained in detail, as will the defensive deployments most effective against the "stall" and the "freeze." The Sliding Zone has been successful in both its active and passive phases, applying pressure or releasing pressure to play a waiting game.

The many diagrams and pictures which appear in the text

will help the reader understand the continuity in teaching defensive maneuvers. The Sliding Zone Defense can help a team overcome an opponent's superior physical skills. It can help minimize the advantage an opponent may have by playing on their home court. It is a defense which allows the coach considerable freedom to re-position or substitute with minimal loss of effectiveness. The Sliding Zone is strictly a team defense, derived from the individual fundamentals of the game of basketball.

John S. Egli

ACKNOWLEDGMENTS

Dr. John D. Lawther, Dean Emeritus, Pennsylvania State University for his encouragement, guidance and advice.

Dr. Elmer A. Gross, Professor of Physical Education, Pennsylvania State University for his encouragement, guidance and advice.

Dr. James D. Gallagher, Assistant Professor of Physical Education, Pennsylvania State University for his encouragement, guidance and advice.

Mr. Phil Bath, Photographer of Bill Russell Photographs.

Sports Illustrated, for providing photographs of Bill Russell.

Mr. Dick Brown, Photographer, *Centre Daily Times*—pictures of zone defense.

Athletic Journal, Parts of 2 Out 3 Back Zone by Dr. John D. Lawther.

Scholastic Coach, Parts of 3 Out 2 Back Zone—Zone Press by Dr. Elmer A. Gross.

Mrs. Sandra Herniman, Typist.

Contents

PART III: ZONE PRESSES—THE ATTACKING DEFENSES

KEY TO DIAGRAMS

Defensive Players: Y̆ Y̆ Y̆ Y̆ Y̆
                      1 2 3 4 5

Offensive Players: Ⓐ Ⓑ Ⓒ Ⓓ Ⓔ

Cut or Slide: ───────────→

Pass: ─ ─ ─ ─ ─→

Dribble: 〜〜〜→

Deflection: ℓℓℓℓℓℓ→

Shot: · · · · · ·>

Rebound: ○ ○ ○ ○ ○ ○>

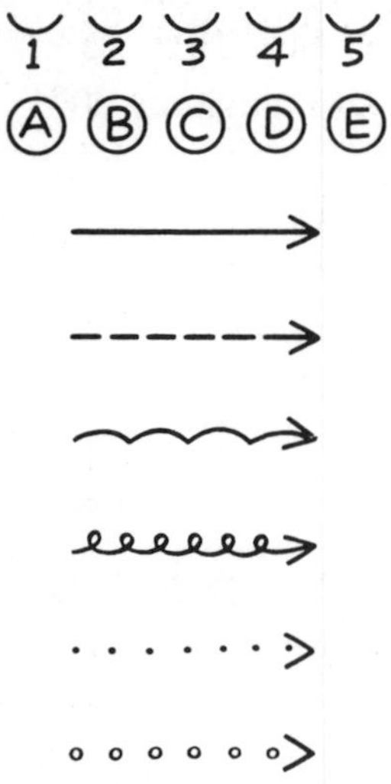

Part I

Development of Zone Defense

1

Foundations of the Sliding Zone Defense

The coach who wishes to establish the Sliding Zone as his primary team defense should first have some understanding of fundamental zone defense. This is essential, for the Sliding Zone is, after all, a type of zone defense which was evolved from several earlier zones to counter the improvements and progressions of offensive tactics. A study of the purposes, strengths, and limitations of various zone defenses enables the coach to see how the Sliding Zone was derived. Only as one develops an insight into the foundations of the Sliding Zone will he be able to understand the flexibility which the Sliding Zone offers and the coaching methods which it requires.

In the early development of zone defense the players were placed in front of the defensive hoop and were assigned certain territories with instructions to concentrate on the movement of the ball. Shifting to new positions was determined by the location of the ball relative to the basket. The general axiom was to try to have at least one defender between the offensive man with the ball and the basket. An offensive player who entered a scoring area, with or without the ball, was guarded

19

in a manner not unlike man-for-man defense. Early zone formations were developed mainly out of necessity. Some coaches discovered that the man-for-man defense was becoming more and more vulnerable to intricate screen or pick plays and that the taller defensive men were often lured away from rebounding position as a result of a "switch" in guarding assignments. There were other factors which made a zone defense an asset, if not a necessity, to a team. These factors included:

1. Short, narrow courts
2. Low ceilings (prevented long shots)
3. Overhanging balconies (prevented corner shots)
4. Poor lighting
5. Lack of standardized equipment
6. Lack of standardized and organized officiating and interpreting of rules
7. The 3-second rule of 1936
8. The offensive charging rule.

The general purposes of zone play have remained basically the same since its inception. Some of these advantages are listed as follows:

1. Reduces the effectiveness of screening or blocking by the offense
2. Leads to a stronger and more consistent defensive rebounding
3. Tends to facilitate pass interceptions
4. Provides for fast-break opportunities
5. Enables strategic positioning of taller and/or slower players
6. Protects against in-close shooting
7. Minimizes the effectiveness of a "driving" team
8. Tends to result in less fouling
9. Develops a feeling for *team* defense
10. Adjusts readily for pressing, sloughing, or overloading purposes.

Many of the advantages of zone defense were offset by the continued development of individual skills in shooting, dribbling, and passing. Other weaknesses of the zone were exploited by sound analyses from within the coaching ranks (National Association of Basketball Coaches was formed in 1927), and by the advent of the wide and long court. Players not only were taught how to "beat the zone" but they now had room enough to do it! Thus, some of the disadvantages of the zone defense should be listed.

1. Weak against side shots and long shots
2. Individual responsibility not as great as when playing man for man
3. Weak against a slow, deliberate attack
4. Weak against a fast break
5. Overall team defense is weak unless shifting as a unit is accomplished
6. One defensive man often has to try to stop two offensive men
7. Difficult to double-team a star player.

The reader should keep in mind that the Sliding Zone was developed to minimize these weaknesses.

EARLIER ZONES

A closer look at some of the specific zone defenses may help conceptualize the foundations of the Sliding Zone.

The Two Out–Three Back Zone. This defense was designed to keep defensive strength near the basket area. The territory to be covered by the two front men was increased. They had to chase harder and cover more territory. This permitted more outside shooting, and often allowed passes to be made into the pivot area around the foul line. Defense in the dangerous area close to the basket was strengthened. The offense was limited to side and long shots as the presence of three men near the basket area made it difficult for the offense to get a close shot, and practically impossible to get a lay-up. In addition the three back players provided excellent rebound strength. Players were assigned specific areas as indicated in Diagram 1.

The Three Out–Two Back Zone. This defense was designed to stop the outside shooters by placing the defensive strength above the foul line as shown in Diagram 2. If the front-line men were able to intercept a pass or grab a long rebound an excellent fast-break opportunity was presented. This defense was found to be weak in the corners and in the center areas around the foul line. Mr. Clair Bee, a pioneer in the development of the zone defense, recommended a rather easy slide to cover the weak areas in the corners and middle.[1] When a back-line man shifted to his near corner, the front-line wing man farthest from the ball shifted to a position under the hoop. The middle man in the front line dropped back in to protect the middle in the three out–two back.

The Two-One-Two Zone. However, in order to facilitate teaching of the Sliding Zone, it may be easier to convert the three out–two back into the two-one-two by moving the middle man of the front line into the center position, rather than using Bee's method. The reasons for this will be more clearly seen in Chapter 4. Diagram 3 shows the areas to be covered by the early two-one-two zone.

The One-Three-One Zone. This type of defense exhibited excellent strength in the middle and under the basket. It was found to be very weak against shots taken from the side or corner. This zone was much more effective when goal tending was permitted by the rules and was very popular during the early 1940's. Today, teams are reluctant to use it because of improved shooting from the sides and corners, along with the enforcement of the goal-tending rule. Diagram 4 shows the

---

[1] Clair Bee, *Zone Defense and Attack* (New York: A. S. Barnes and Company, Inc., 1942), pp. 9–10.

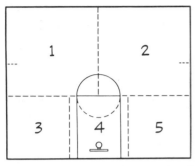

Diagram 1. Two Out–Three Back.

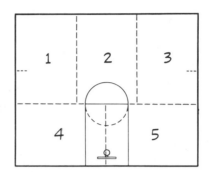

Diagram 2. Three Out–Two Back.

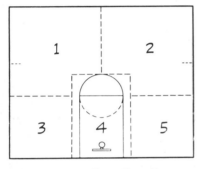

Diagram 3. Two-One-Two.

Diagram 4. One-Three-One.

one-three-one formation. You will be shown later how this is one of the formations incorporated into the three out–two back Sliding Zone. When the ball is in the middle, the three out– two back assumes practically the same setup with a few minor adjustments. (See diagram 105 and photo 12.)

The Three-One-One Zone. This particular zone allowed shots to be attempted from difficult angles on the side, corner, and out front. This defense was rather weak against an over-load, particularly if the offense had a good passer and play maker out front feeding the ball to the forwards. Slides from this defense were relatively simple, with the front men drop-ping straight back. The man playing at the foul line would drop toward the hoop when #5 would be pulled to the corner.

The move to the corner was too long for #5 to get there and prevent the shot. It did not become popular as a basic defense. However, it is one of the formations incorporated into the three out–two back basic Sliding Zone Defense and is very applicable for half court presses and for defending against the stall (see Chapters 9 and 10). Diagram 5 shows the basic three-one-one zone.

The One-Two-Two and Two-Two-One Zones. Two other basic formations which helped in the evolving of the Sliding Zone were the one-two-two zone, Diagram 6, and the two-two-one zone, Diagram 7.

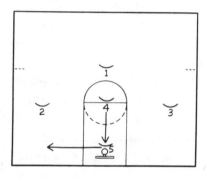

Diagram 5. Three-One-One.

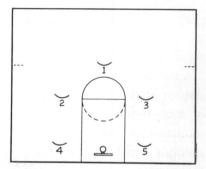

Diagram 6. One-Two-Two.

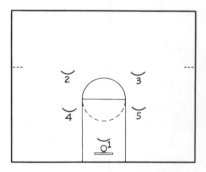

Diagram 7. Two-Two-One.

The one-two-two zone allowed the point man or #1 to chase and harass out front. The weaknesses were along the sides, corner, and middle. It appeared to be similar to the three out–two back setup. The two-two-one zone was employed to have the #1 man act as the goal tender, again in present day basketball, goal tending is less effective. However, today one must admit the professionals use their biggest man in this position, as do many college and high school teams. It is a great place for the giant. The two-one-two Sliding Zone (see Chapter 5) utilizes these two formations. This defense shows a resemblance to the box-and-one and diamond-and-one defenses.

Thus, the various straight zone defenses became obsolete as player and coaching skills, equipment, facilities and officiating gradually changed and improved. The innovations in zone defense play, which then came about through the efforts of coaches such as Clair Bee, John Lawther, Cam Henderson, and Arthur Shabinger, are responsible for some of the many systems of zone defense in vogue today. The Sliding Zone is indeed a modern-day zone defense. It has combined proven zone fundamentals and basic man-for-man coverage with original sliding techniques.

2

Teaching the Sliding Zone

Before a coach attempts to teach the Sliding Zone he should familiarize himself with the general theories of basic zone play discussed in Chapter 1. He must then recognize that no matter what formation or style of defense his team uses, successful execution still depends on how well his players learn proper defensive stance, pivoting, balance, proper use of arms and hands, and purposeful footwork. No defensive arrangement and strategy can overcome sloppy fundamental preparation. Efforts to improve these fundamental skills can easily become an integral part of drills specifically planned to teach components of the Sliding Zone.

A thorough analysis of the Sliding Zone by the coach is needed. He should discover that many of the straight zone defenses are actually parts of the Sliding Zone and that a continuity of change from one type of zone to another is possible by predetermined slides. Such an analysis will enable the coach also to "break down" the Sliding Zone into smaller teachable units (sometimes referred to as meaningful wholes). The Sliding Zone is complex and needs a carefully planned progression of drills and routines for efficient learning. A recommended procedure for teaching the mechanics of the Sliding Zone follows.

INDIVIDUAL FUNDAMENTALS

The One-Against-One. This fundamental situation when understood reveals a basic advantage for the offense (as do the basic rules and principles of modern-day basketball and their interpretations). For example: the most basic situation of the game itself is "one-against-one." In this situation the player with the ball, the offensive man, has the advantage because he knows what he is going to do with the ball and when he is going to do it. Therefore, the defensive man is at a disadvantage and must wait until the offensive man has started his action before responding with a defensive move. If the defensive man anticipates the move of the offensive man and guesses incorrectly, or if he is misled by a "faking maneuver," he will be pulled out of position and beaten.

The one-on-one drill setup illustrated in Diagram 8 is executed several times at every practice session early in the season. It need not be used as often later in the season. The coach should be the judge of when to run it.

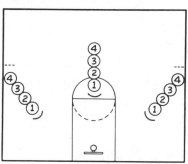

Diagram 8.   One-on-One Drill.

In the drill in Diagram 8, we form three lines as shown. The "O" represents the offense. The "U" represents the defensive man at the head of the line. The offensive man (1) with the ball drives around the defensive man and tries to score. The offensive man should drive from each position shown; left side, center, and right side. He should take at least two turns from each position driving around the defensive man both left and right from each line. Then the defensive man should go to the rear of any of the lines. The coach should have the defensive man covering use the proper techniques of "near-arm guarding" and "windmilling." After taking his turn the defensive man should go to the rear of the line and let another man play the defensive position, thus permitting each squad member the opportunity to play the defensive position. If the techniques of "near-arm guarding" and "windmilling" are mastered by the players, perhaps the drill should then only be used as a review. This is very rough work and the players should be protected against injuries as much as possible.

Near Arm Guarding. This technique is incorporated into the one-on-one situation used as a basic part of the Sliding Zone. The explanation of this type of guarding is as follows: If the offensive man tries to drive around the defensive man's right, the defensive man must pivot on his rear foot, either left or right, toward the offensive man and slide along with the offensive man. At the same time he brings his left hip alongside of the offensive man and raises his left hand over the defensive man's head. The left hand becomes the near hand and is closer to the ball when it is released for a shot. In this way the left hand has a better chance of deflecting the ball than the right hand.

The technique of near-arm guarding in the one-on-one situation is demonstrated by Bill Russell in the picture sequence beginning with Photo 1. Russell is considered the greatest defensive player of all time and he deserves this title. As you observe Bill in these pictures you can see how well he has mas-

Photo 1. Number 32 has started his drive past Bill Russell (#6) who has made his pivot and is beginning to stride along with #32 (bringing his left hip and left hand alongside of the offensive man).

Photo 2. Number 32 is ready to release his shot. Russell (#6) is striding alongside and bringing his left arm and hand up towards the ball.

Photo 3.   **Number 32 releases the ball, Russell leaves his feet bringing his left hand up to the ball and into position to deflect it.**

Photo 4. This photo shows Bill Russell with the full extension of his left arm, with his left hand on the ball ready to deflect it away from the hoop. His left hip is making contact with the back side of #32. This contact by the hip will minimize the possibility of injury to the defender.

33

Photo 5.   This shows the follow-through of Russell's left hand guiding the ball safely away from the hoop.

Photo 6.   This shows Bill Russell (#6) at the completion of the
defensive maneuver of near-arm guarding in the one-on-one situation, and preparing to make contact with the floor.

tered this fundamental of defensive basketball. It is the opinion of the author that these pictures, illustrating the proper near-arm guarding technique, are a classic.* One should remember, if the offensive man decides to drive to his right, the defensive player must reverse this procedure and do everything to his right side.

Windmilling. When an offensive player starts a drive to his right then changes and goes left our defensive man windmills; that is, he turns and pivots to his right with his left hand up. As the offensive man changes direction and goes to his right, the defensive man drops his left hand, steps toward the offensive man with his right arm up and right hip in, causing a "windmill" motion or change of direction. Remember, this procedure is reversed if the offensive player starts a drive to his left then changes and goes right.

Two-on-One. This brings into play basic fundamentals involving two teammates. One should progress from the "individual" offensive maneuvers of the "one-on-one" situation to the "two-on-one" situation. After the individual fundamentals have been mastered, plan to use them in meeting the various situations which are common to the game of basketball and involve more than one man. The first of these situations is two offensive men against one defensive man. In this situation it is the object of the two offensive men to stay wide and then work in as close to the hoop as possible in order to get a good shot (see Diagram 9).

The assignment of the defensive man #1 is more difficult—he employs a delaying action called fake-and-fade. This is done by the defensive man faking toward the offensive man with the ball, "A," at the top of the foul circle and trying to stop his dribbling or cutting movements. The defender then fades, or drops back, between the foul line and the dotted line to

---

* These pictures were taken by Mr. Phil Bath and first published in *Sports Illustrated.*

prevent or break up a pass to the other offensive man, "B." He definitely tries to prevent "B" from getting a lay-up by getting between him and the basket. Defensive man #1 also tries to delay the offense until the second defensive man (#2) can get back and pick up "A." If defensive man #1 is fortunate or skillful enough to intercept the ball or delay the offense until help arrives, he has done his part in preventing a score.

GROUP FUNDAMENTALS

Two-on-Two. This situation evolves from the two-on-one and brings into play the development of the offensive fundamental of screening. Theoretically, two defensive men cannot stop two offensive men from scoring. The main reasons are: (1) because of the previously mentioned fact of "head start" of the offensive man in the one-on-one situation, and (2) because of the fundamental of screening.

Diagrams 10, 11, 12, and 13 illustrate the fundamental of screening.

Diagram 10 shows the offensive player "A," who has the ball, passing to "B" who is moving out to meet the ball and set the screen.

As "B" catches the ball he turns and faces the hoop with his back to "A" and defensive man #1. Then "A" fakes to his left and cuts right passing "B" so closely that defensive man #1 cannot run with him and get between "A" and "B"—thus executing the screen (see Diagram 11). Number 1 has to delay or run the longer route to the outside of "B" (see Diagram 12).

This is actually a form of "blocking"; however, "screening" is the term used in the official basketball rules, and a "screen" in order to be legal must be executed according to the rules.[1]

---

[1] *Official NCAA Basketball Guide 1969.* Official Rules, page 21, Rule 4, Section 25: A Screen is legal action by a player who, without causing contact, delays or prevents an opponent from reaching a desired position.

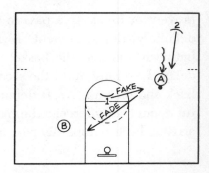

Diagram 9. Two-on-One. Next defensive man down court picks up offensive man "A."

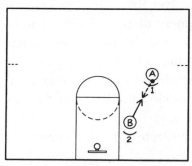

Diagram 10.
Moving to Meet Ball.

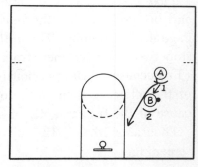

Diagram 11.
"B" Screening #1.

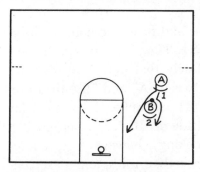

Diagram 12.
Outside Route by #1.

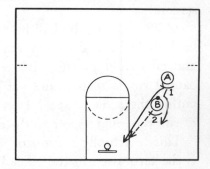

Diagram 13.
Pass, "B" to "A".

As "A" goes by "B," the screen man, "A" should be open for a return pass from "B" and should have a clear path to the goal (see Diagram 13).

The screening maneuver points out a definite advantage for the offensive team. If the defensive men try to stay with their men, this fundamental of "screening" when properly executed, will beat the defense.

Diagrams 14, 15, and 16 illustrate and explain the "switching" fundamental by the defense and the offensive fundamental of "rolling off" or "splitting" the switch.

In Diagram 14, the "switch" takes place and is executed by defensive men #1 and #2. When #2 sees that #1 is screened out, #2 yells "switch" and picks up offensive man "A" as he cuts off the screen set by "B." Number 1 automatically slips in from his outside position and picks up "B," completing the defensive switch.

However, another counter action by the offensive men may then take place. This is the previously mentioned fundamental of "rolling off" or "splitting" the switch.

Diagram 15 illustrates the "roll," or "splitting" the switch. For a brief instant, defensive man #1 will be on the outside of offensive man "B" as "B" passes to "A" cutting past. Now, as defensive man #2 switches to pick up "A" as he is going for the hoop, "B" will have a clear opening for the near corner of the backboard. Thus, #1 will not be able to get between "B" and the basket in time to stop a return pass from "A" or to prevent "B" from then shooting or driving to the goal for a lay-up (see Diagram 16).

Therefore, the fundamentals of "screening" and "splitting" or "rolling" off the switch favor the offensive men, making it very difficult to defend with a straight man for man.

These fundamentals of basketball have been highly developed. With the addition of three more players to make a team of five men, an infinite number of screens become possible.

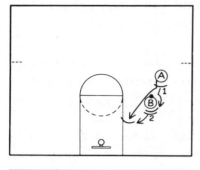

Diagram 14.
#2 Switching to "A".
#1 Switching to "B".

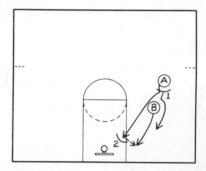

Diagram 15.   #2 Switching to Pick Up "A"; Path Opens for "B"
to Roll or Split.

Diagram 16.   Shows #2 on "A"—"B" Open on Split or Roll.

Three-on-Two. From these fundamentals we progress to the situation of three-on-two; three offensive men against two defensive men. The offensive men not only have the previously discussed benefits working for them, but also the obvious advantage of having an extra man. Theoretically, the offensive men should score when they are in this situation (shown in Diagram 17).

The three-on-two situation often occurs as the climax to a successful fast break; the "break" principle is to try to get the defense into an outnumbered situation. The three-on-two occurs at times during play, not only on the fast break, but also as a result of successful screening or sharp changes of

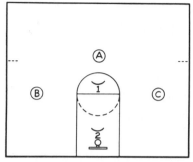

Diagram 17. Three-on-Two.

direction in the offensive team's pattern. The three-on-two drill is used by practically every basketball team and is considered to be one of the most important drills used in perfecting both offensive and defensive maneuvers. The author considers the defensive phase of this drill to be the backbone of the Sliding Zone Defense.

In the utilization of this drill we combine man-for-man defensive techniques with defensive shifting to specific areas according to the location of the ball and playing both the man and the ball. One of the most important jobs in teaching the Sliding Zone Defense is to familiarize the players with the unfamiliar sliding movements and to break them of the habit of guarding one particular man on defense.

The three-on-two drill "setup," shown in Diagram 18, is used for this purpose. In this drill three offensive men, "A," "B," and "C," attempt to score against two defensive men, #1 and #2.

Offensive player "A" takes a position at the top of the foul circle, "B" positions himself halfway between the basket and the left sideline, and "C" assumes a position halfway between the basket and the right sideline. Defensive man #1 takes the man with the ball, "A," while #2 takes a position in front of the basket and midway between the other two offensive men, "B" and "C."

Defensive man #2's job is to guard the offensive man "B" or "C," whoever receives the pass from "A." When "A" passes to "B," as shown in Diagram 18, #2 quickly slides into a de-

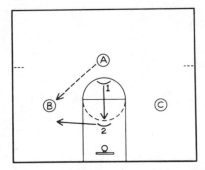 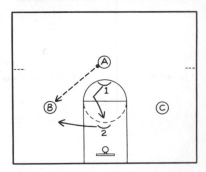

Diagram 18.   Pass, "A" to "B" Covered by #2.

Diagram 19.   Incorrect Move by #1.

fensive position between "B" and the basket. Player #1 moves his left foot backward as he faces the direction of the pass and quickly slides into a position halfway between "A" and "C." His job is to guard either man "A" or "C," whoever receives the ball from "B."

A very serious error is often committed by defensive man #1: the defensive players in this position have a tendency to move toward the first pass and follow the ball as it is passed from "A" to "B" (see Diagram 19).

This out-of-the-way move will consume just enough time to prevent #1 from arriving at the midway point soon enough to execute his next defensive move. Remember, he can get to the midway point on time *only* if he takes his first step straight back. On each succeeding pass, one defensive man will always take the offensive man who receives the ball while the other defensive man will take a position near the basket between the other two offensive men who are in position to receive a pass.

The three offensive players must remember to keep spread in a triangular formation or the two defensive men will stop them.

Diagrams 20, 21, 22 and 23 illustrate the possible combinations of passes and slides, the letters indicate the defensive

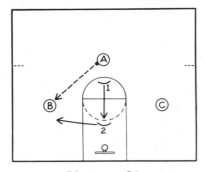

Diagram 20.
Pass: "A" to "B"
Slide: #1——#2.

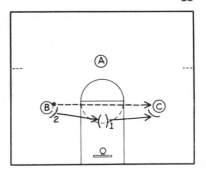

Diagram 21.
Pass: "B" to "C"
Slide: #1 Covers "C"
and #2 Slides to Position
Vacated by #1.

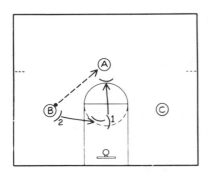

Diagram 22.
Pass: "B"——"A"
Slide: #1 Covers "A,"
#2 Slides to Position
Vacated by #1 and Faces "A."

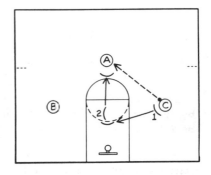

Diagram 23.
Pass: "C"——"A"
Slide: #2 Moves Out and
Covers "A"—#1 Slides into
Position Vacated by #2 and
Faces "A" with Ball.

men who should slide into which defensive position.

The three-on-two drill is the foundation of the Sliding Zone Defense. We feel it is most essential in teaching the Sliding Zone Defense for the coach to be well versed in the drills we have just discussed. They are definitely the heart and soul of the Sliding Zone Defense, and they will play a very essential

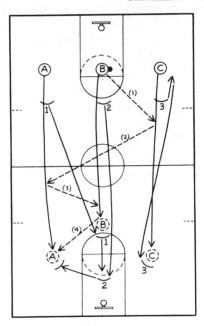

Diagram 24.   Pass: "B"——"C"——"A"——"B"——"A." #3 delays by touching foul line extended, before he may retreat and come back for defense, to a position where he can pick up loose man "C."

part in the makeup of the five man defense which will follow.

Three-on-Three. We have developed a full-court drill which aids in the transition of offense to defense. It is a full-court drill involving three-on-three from a moving three-on-two.

This drill sets up as shown in Diagram 24 with offensive men "A," "B," and "C" in the positions shown ready to attack down court and try to get a 3 on 2 situation at the conclusion of a fast break. The defensive men lined up in front of and facing the offensive men are #1, #2, and #3. The coach can call out any one of the three defensive numbers. This is the signal for the offense to start down court and for the other two defensive men whose numbers were not called to immediately retreat to their defensive positions in the 3 on 2 situation. The defensive man whose number was called must delay by going forward and touching the foul line extended, then retreat to the defensive end of the court where he will pick up the loose offensive man. Numbers 1 and 2 will be playing 2 against 3, fighting a delaying action until #3 who has delayed can get back and pick up the loose man. This, then, sets up a 3 on 3 situation.

The fundamentals we have just explained all illustrate definite advantages of the offense over the defense. With the 3 on 2 situation of offense outnumbering defense, we feel the defense tends to get better results by combining man-for-man techniques with intelligent defensive shifting to specific areas. These areas are determined according to where the ball is located in reference to the defensive hoop. Here we must play both the man and the ball. We know if abilities of the players are *equally* matched one defensive man cannot stop one offensive man; two defensive men cannot stop two offensive men; and of course, two defensive men cannot stop three offensive men. We do know, however, that by practicing and stressing the defensive moves of the 3 on 2 situation, the defensive men will become so *efficient* in executing the defensive slides that they will become successful in stopping the three men. One thing is certain, by executing these moves correctly, two men can always bother three men and perhaps force them to take a bad shot, just as one defensive man can bother and often prevent one offensive man from scoring. The same degree of effectiveness applies also for two against two, three against three, four against four, and five against five.

Other defensive fundamentals relative to zone rebounding, area responsibilities, and defensive signaling or "touching-off" will be discussed later.

Part II

Basic Zone Defense Formations

3

Two Out—Three Back Sliding Zone

The 2 out 3 back sliding zone defense is designed to keep defensive strength back near the basket area, while at the same time keeping enough pressure on the outside offensive men to force them into taking hurried shots over the defensive men's hands. This will also force the offense to make errant passes which can be intercepted. This defense is our basic defense—it contains every move which will be discussed in the other defensive alignments. If a coach and/or player masters this basic 2 out 3 back defense the remaining defenses will be much more easily understood. We consider this defense to be our "passive defense," that is, we stay back, keeping enough pressure on the offense to force the bad shot or errant pass and then from our strong position near the board retrieve the ball. If we get a steal, long rebound, or interception, we will of course fast break. We do not consider this to be an attack or active defense. It is very good for utilizing players who do not have exceptional basketball talents, such as speed and quickness, and it is the greatest defense for big kids not brilliant but smart and possessing a lot of desire and hustle. It is also an excellent defense against a team which is poor at shooting from the outside.

SELECTION OF PERSONNEL

The selection of personnel to fit into the front and back line is important, particularly if you, as a coach, are in a position where you can choose these players. This is the ideal situation; however, if you have to make use of the material on hand, the following selection-of-personnel chart should be of value in the eventual placement of the players so that a coach may get the maximum performance from these players. We have found that players with the qualifications listed on the next page have made this defense successful.

PRINCIPLES TO REMEMBER

In teaching the Sliding Zone Defense one should be aware of the fact that the 2 out 3 back formation is the basic foundation for this defense. This is imperative! We stress each defensive man's remembering that every time the ball is moved, passed, dribbled, or shot he *automatically* slides to a certain position on the court relative to the position of the ball and the basket area. The defensive players must be properly indoctrinated for playing this type of defense; they must be alert, aggressive, and have a lot of desire. It is strictly a team defense requiring the utmost in teamwork, and it must be practiced daily so it can be applied at its best. It will not work unless each player cooperates through talking and working together. Talking must be done intelligently in order to help one another. For example: the player should let his teammates know what he is doing by talking loudly enough and saying,

(Position #1)

1. Can be a small man
2. Must be very active
3. Must possess a lot of energy and hustle
4. Must be able to handle fast break
5. Able to use either hand
6. A satisfactory dribbler
7. Good right hand shooter-off-the-drive when fast breaking
8. Good at retrieving loose balls and the medium-long rebound

(Position #2)

1. Should possess the same qualities as #1
2. Should be a good left hand shooter-off-the-drive when fast breaking

(Position #3 — left)

1. Should be second biggest man, tall, strong and rugged
2. Should be able to rebound while on the move and crash the boards hard
3. Adequate ball handler and dribbler to help with the fast break
4. Should be agile and quick enough to make the move from foul line extended to the far side of the board
5. Must have enough fortitude to battle the biggest men of the opposing team

(Position #4)

1. Should be the biggest, strongest man you have
2. Rugged, hard working
3. Good rebounder from standing position
4. Must be good at boxing out and getting rebound position
5. Must be a good passer with one hand or both hands for clearing ball to start fast break

(Position #3 — right)

1. Same qualities as #5
2. Should be good ball handler and dribbler
3. Good right-hand shooter and driver

"I'm Up," or "I'm Back," or "I've Got the Ball," "I've Got the Post," or "Middle," "Side," or "Corner." These audible signals are important in aiding the players in making their slides to the next position more quickly.

An example of unintelligent talking is when a defensive man tells an offensive man to go ahead and shoot. This type of talking becomes even more *unintelligent* for the defense when the offensive man makes the shot.

BASIC TWO OUT—THREE BACK SLIDES

The following diagrams illustrate the basic slides of the five men employing the 2 out 3 back Sliding Zone Defense. There are two starting positions for the front-line men (#1 and #2). These positions are the key to this defense and they must be assumed quickly and correctly so that the defensive strength of the back line will be "swung" toward the ball, from where the offensive attack must come. One position is referred to as the "UP" position, and the other is the "BACK" position.

Starting Position 1. Diagram 25 shows the starting position when the ball is at B in the area of #1. This is referred to as the "UP POSITION" of the front line. Number 2 takes a position straddling the foul circle, about one step in front of the foul line on the left side. Number 3 takes the "UP POSITION" (of the back line) halfway between the foul circle and the right sideline with his feet on an imaginary line (foul line extended). The "UP" positions of #1 and #3 are very important, and they must be taken in order to protect the open area immediately accessible to the offense in the area of the ball. These up positions also determine the forthcoming moves of the other defensive men. Number 4 will take a position with his left foot on the dotted line of the foul circle and his right foot on the right foul-lane line, and #5 will position himself about a step back of the dotted line of the foul circle and straddle the left lane line.

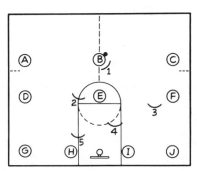

Diagram 25.
Starting Position #1 with #1 Up.

Starting Position 2. Diagram 26 shows the starting position when the ball is at B and #2 takes the front line "UP POSITION." This permits #1 to drop back on the right side. It then becomes imperative for #5 stationed on the back line on the left to assume the "UP" position for the back line. Numbers 4 and 3 only have to move about one-and-a-half steps to their new positions.

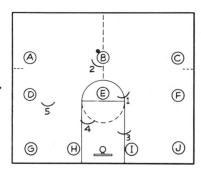

Diagram 26.
Starting Position #1 with #2 Up.

Photo 7. This illustrates the 2 out 3 back sliding zone, starting position #1 with front-line man #30 "UP," and back-line man #50 (number not visible) in the "UP" position. This photograph corresponds to Diagram 26.

Back-Line Position. The "UP" positions of the front line are determined by the style of play being used by the offensive team. If the offensive team continually brings the ball down the left side and into the right side of the defense, we have found it best to bring #2 to the UP position and drop #1 back on the right. This makes the back-line slides less complicated, particularly in the case where the offense is using a three or four man overload (see Diagram 27).

If the offensive team is first challenged by #1 who assumes the "UP" position and the offensive team works the ball down the right side, this creates a lot more activity for the back line. If #2 is "UP" and the offensive team works the ball to the left side, the back line is compelled to make longer slides. The defense must be alert at all times in order to adjust and play the strength of the offense. If the two front men are confronted with the offense bringing the ball directly and precisely down the middle of the court (shown by the dotted line), one of the "UP" men must commit himself and take the man with the ball.

By scouting your opponent you can determine which side they will most often bring the ball down. If you do not have a chance to scout your opponent, we have found it to be true, by keeping statistics, that a team will bring the ball down on their right side of the court about 85 percent of the time. This means you should have the left side of your defense ready to *shift* or *slide* to meet this challenge. When sliding into position, the back-line men must assume their "UP" positions quickly. Remember this very important rule: if the front man is "UP" on the *right* side of your defense, the back-line man on the *same* side (right) is automatically the *"UP"* man of the *back line*. The same principle applies to the left side. This is a very important move and must be mastered or the following defensive moves will be of no avail.

Diagram 27 depicts #2 playing the ball, allowing #1 to

drop back and play the pass to "C" or "F" against an overload. This will permit #3 and #4 to play their positions without moving very much. *Note*: As #2 takes the "UP" position on the right side of the court, #5 must assume the "UP" position for the back line on the left side.

These moves just discussed are very simple. They lead into the basic slides which comprise the sliding zone defense.

Defensive Coverage on All Possible Passing Plays. Diagram

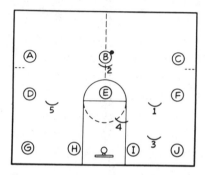

Diagram 27.   Starting Position #2.

Photo 8. This illustrates the 2 out 3 back sliding zone, starting position #2 with front-line man #30 (number not visible) coming over to the right side of the court, and still remaining in the "UP" position. Front-line man #34 stays back, even though the ball is on his side of the court. Back-line man #50 (number partially visible) is in the "UP" position. This photo corresponds to Diagram 27.

28 illustrates the defensive slides when the ball is passed from
"B" to "F." Number 3 moves into a defensive guarding position
between the ball handler "F" and the basket while #1 slides
to a position along the right side of the foul line just outside
the lane to prevent a pass into "E" at the high post. Number
4 slides to a position halfway between the center of the foul
line and the right corner of the court, and #5 moves to a position directly in front of the hoop with his left foot near the
dotted line of the foul circle. Number 2 turns to his right facing
the ball and places his right foot on the foul line near the left
side of the lane. When the ball is at "F" the defensive alignment should be as shown in Diagram 29.

Illustrated in Diagram 30 are the defensive slides when the
ball is passed from "F" to "J."

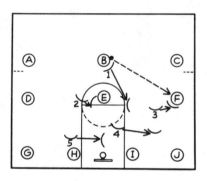

Diagram 28.
Pass: "B"——"F"

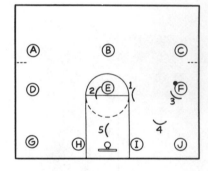

Diagram 29.

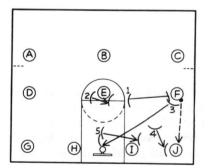

Diagram 30.
Pass: "F"——"J."

Number 4 slides to the corner and covers "J." Number 3 pivots toward the hoop facing the ball and drives for the far side of the backboard, and as he drives and reaches a point between "J" in the corner and "E" in the high post he watches for a pass from "J" to "E." Number 5 moves to a position outside the foul lane where he can pick up "J" if he drives around #4 or if "J" passes to "I." Number 4 is in a position to play "I" or to prevent or intercept the pass. Number 2 turns facing the ball and takes a position at the center of the foul line; his main job is to keep the ball out of the high post, keeping alert so he can move out front and guard "B" or "A" if the ball should go back out to either of these men. Number 2 must be careful so as not to get screened in by "E" at the high post while #3 continues on his drive toward the board and takes the position originally occupied by #5 directly in front of the hoop.

A very important defensive maneuver is executed here requiring teamwork and cooperation between numbers 3 and 5. If #5 decides to take "I" he must let #3 know, for example, by hollering, "I've got 'I.'" This alerts #3 so that he may continue on through to the position in front of the hoop. However, if #3, as he is driving back toward the hoop, can cover "I," #5 does not have to leave his position in front of the hoop and he will not have to move at all. In turn this will cut down the length of #3's slide, making this maneuver much quicker and less complicated. Remember, if the pass from "J" to "I" is too fast for #3 to cover "I," then #5 must take "I" and #3 will continue on through toward the board and take the original position held by #5. At the same time, #1 moves to a position along the right sideline at "F" where he looks for any pass coming out on this side of the court. If "J" decides to drive to his right with a dribble around #4, then #1 moves in and "joins" "J" along with #4 and both #1 and #4 try to tie up "J."

The defensive alignment after these moves have been executed is shown in Diagrams 31 and 32.

If "J" passes to "I" in either Diagrams 31 or 32, there are two possible defensive coverages on "I." Diagram 33 shows #3 guarding "I" and Diagram 34 shows #5 guarding "I."

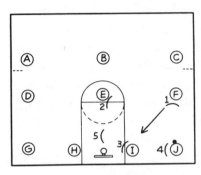

Diagram 31.
Shows #3 Covering "I" and
#5 Holding in Front of Hoop.

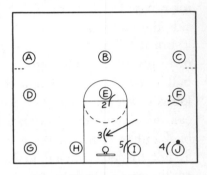

Diagram 32.
Shows #5 Taking "I" and #3
Driving for and Taking the
Position in Front of the
Hoop which Was Vacated by #5.

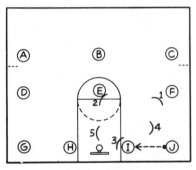

Diagram 33.
Pass: "J"——"I"

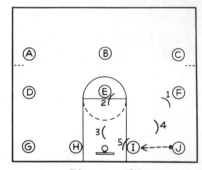

Diagram 34.
Pass: "J"——"I"

When the pass is made from "J" to "I," #2 maintains his position at the foul line. Numbers 1 and 4 turn in facing the ball and the hoop, moving towards the hoop to tighten up the defense around the ball.

If "I" passes to "H" on the other side of the foul line (Diagram 35), and #3 is covering "I," the moves are as follows:

As "I" passes to "H" (when #3 is guarding "I") #5 will slide over and guard "H" on the other side of the foul lane. Number 3 will turn toward the pass and take the position in front of the hoop, which was just vacated by #5. Number 4 will slide in front of "I" into the position vacated by #3, and #2 will slide to his right and out toward the sideline. Number 1 will move to his right to a position straddling the right foul-lane line with his right foot on the foul line.

The defensive alignment with the ball at "H" and #5 covering "H" is shown in Diagram 36.

The defensive slides when the ball is passed from "H" to "G" are shown in Diagram 37.

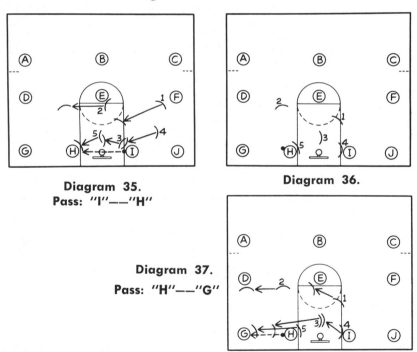

Diagram 35.
Pass: "I"——"H"

Diagram 36.

Diagram 37.
Pass: "H"——"G"

When "H" passes to "G," defensive man #5 who was guarding "H" goes with the pass to the corner and covers "G." Number 3 moves halfway between the hoop and the corner

and in front of "H," while #4 moves to the position vacated by
#3 in front of the hoop and faces the ball in the corner. Num-
ber 2 will slide to his right and along the left sideline looking
for any pass out in his area from "G." Number 1 should automatically move to the left side of the foul line near the lane line
with his right foot on the foul line and face the ball in the
corner.

Diagram 34 shows the defensive alignment with #5 covering
"I." If in this situation the ball is passed from "I" to "H" with
#5 covering "I," defensive man #3 should cover "H" and #5
will take #3's vacated position in front of the hoop. Numbers
4, 2, and 1 will execute the moves as they were illustrated in
Diagrams 35, 36, and 37. If the pass is made from "H" to "G"
with #3 covering "H," #3 must execute the move to the
corner, the same as #5 did in Diagram 37. This interchanging
of men in the back line is very important to the success of the
Sliding Zone Defense, and as you can easily see, it is of utmost
importance for the back-line men to learn every position. Our
back-line drill is vital in teaching these men all of the moves
required to play every position, and this drill is given in detail
at the close of this chapter.

Coverage of the post man by the far guard is one of the most
important and effective moves employed in the 2 out 3 back
Sliding Zone Defense. We have a simple but effective rule
which our back-line men must master: when the ball comes
from out front to the side, into the post, the far guard (or back-
line man) takes the post. Diagram 38 shows the execution of
this maneuver.

With the ball at "C" and #1 "UP" to take him, the defensive
alignment should be as shown in Diagram 38. As the pass is
made from "C" to "F," the defensive slides should be as shown
in Diagram 39.

As the pass is made from "C" to "F," #1 leaves "C" and slides
facing the ball toward the foul line. Number 3 slides to his

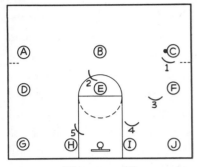

Diagram 38.

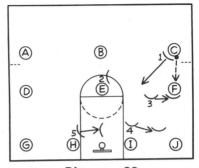

Diagram 39.
Pass: "C"——"F"

right for an easy pickup on "F" and #4 slides to a position halfway between the center of the foul line and the right corner of the court. Number 5 takes a position directly in front of the hoop with his left foot on the dotted line and faces the ball. Number 2 takes his position at the top of the foul circle and straddles the circle line there.

Diagram 40 shows the position of the defense when the ball is at "F" with #1 on his way back toward the foul circle.

As a pass is made from "F" to "E" the slides are executed as shown in Diagram 41.

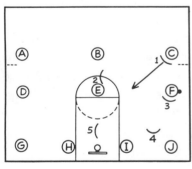

Diagram 40.

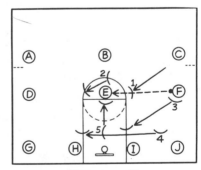

Diagram 41.
Pass: "F"——"E"

In this case, #5, who is called the far guard of the back line, just takes one step toward "E" and covers him. Number 4 of the back line moves as the pass is made to a position on the left side of the lane in front of "H." This appears to be an impossible move as you look at it in the diagram. However, we can assure you that if #4 moves as "F" passes the ball, #4 will be in this position as "E" catches the ball. This will put #4 in an excellent position to cover the left side of the court. Number 2 drops to the left side of the foul line and is ready to move out front or to the left side. Number 1 will continue to drive back for a position near the right side of the foul line, and #3 will slide back facing the ball and take the place left vacant by #4.

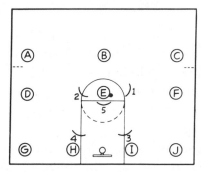

Diagram 42.

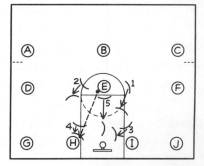

Diagram 43.
Pass: "E"——"H"

Diagram 42 shows the defensive alignment with the ball at "E."

Diagram 43 shows the slides when a pass is made from "E" to "H." As the pass is made, #4 turns and takes "H," #5 drops straight back toward the hoop, #3 moves along the foul lane facing the ball, #1 turns and moves toward the foul lane, and #2 faces in toward the hoop and off to the side of the lane.

Diagram 44 illustrates the defensive alignment when the pass is made from "B" out front directly into the post man "E" when #1 is covering "B."

As "B" passes to "E" at the post, #2 tries to prevent the ball from getting to "E." IF "E" gets the ball, #4 must come up and cover him. Then #1 starts to slide back to a position just outside and at the top of the foul line. Number 5 should be

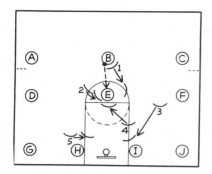

Diagram 44.
Pass: "B"——"E"

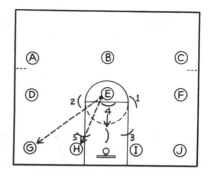

Diagram 45.
Pass: "E"——"G" or "H"

straddling the left lane line and #3 should straddle the right lane line as shown. Number 2 will then help #4 try to tie up "E."

Passes from "E" to "G," or "H," are relatively simple moves and are shown in Diagram 45.

When the pass is made from "E" to "G" or "H," #5 must cover whichever one gets the ball first. Number 4 will drop straight back and if #5 has taken "G" in the corner, he will move to the position in front of "H" as shown in Diagram 46. However, if the pass goes from "E" to "H," it is a simple move for #5 to turn and take "H" with #4 dropping straight back toward the hoop. Number 3 then turns along the lane line facing the ball, and numbers 1 and 2 will move in closer to the hoop.

The positions of all five men when the ball is passed from "E" to "G" are shown in Diagram 46.

Diagram 47 shows coverage when the ball is passed from "E" to "H." Number 5 covers "H" and the other four men take positions as shown and face the ball.

The positions of all five men when the ball is passed from "E" to "I" are shown in Diagram 48. Number 3 covers "I" and the other four men take positions as shown and face the ball.

Diagram 49 illustrates the defensive coverage when the ball

is passed from "E" to "J." The procedure is the same as shown in Diagram 46, only on the right side of the court.

One of the most effective moves executed by the front men is illustrated in Diagram 50. We have found that many interceptions are made as a direct result of this move. When the ball is passed from "J" in the corner out to "F" along the sideline, #1 slides toward the right sideline in front of "F." This places #1 in an excellent position for an interception of the pass from "J" to "F." The other men in the defense retain just about the same positions as shown in Diagram 49. The only difference is that they are facing the ball at "F" as shown in Diagram 50.

If the ball is passed from "F" to "C," the defensive slides are as follows. Number 1 moves along with the pass and covers "C," #2 slides to the front of the foul circle with his right hand in front of "E" between "C" and "E," #3 moves to the "UP" position halfway between the right sideline and the foul line where it joins the foul-lane line on the right side. This defensive

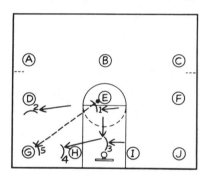

Diagram 46.
Pass: "E"——"G"

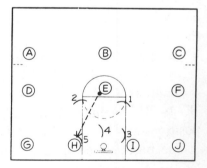

Diagram 47.
Pass: "E"——"H"

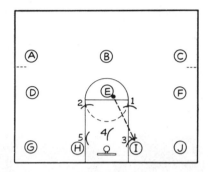

Diagram 48.
Pass: "E"——"I"

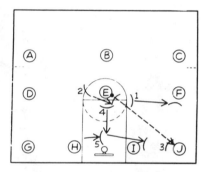

Diagram 49.
Pass: "E"——"J"

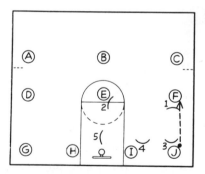

Diagram 50.
Pass: "J"——"F"

Photo 9. This photo illustrates a pass from the corner back out to the side with #34 in position to make the interception or cutoff play. This photo corresponds to Diagram 50.

man will move up as far as the foul line if it were extended to the right sideline. Number 4's position is halfway between the right corner and the center of the foul line, and #5 is directly in front of the hoop with his left foot about six inches from the dotted line part of the foul circle. This is all depicted in Diagram 51.

Any pass from along the baseline out front to "A," "B," "C," "D," or "F" should be covered by a front-line man, either #1 or #2. The coverage on "F" was explained in Diagram 50. If the pass is executed on the other side of the court between "G" and "D," the defensive moves are the same on the left-hand side as they were on the right with #2 being the key man in the defensive moves. If the ball is passed from the baseline to "C," #1 is the most logical man to cover the "C" position, with #2 covering at the top of the foul circle as shown in Diagram 51. If the ball should go to "A" from along the base-line, #2 should slide to cover "A" and #1 will move to the top of the circle with his left hand in front of "E" and between "E" and "F." Number 5 will come to the "UP" position on the left, #4 will slide to the halfway position, and #3 slides to the position in front of the hoop near the dotted line. This maneuver by all of the defensive men looks difficult; however, if the defense is doing its job—by that we mean forcing the high pass out—this will give the defensive men plenty of time to set up their new defensive positioning on the other side of

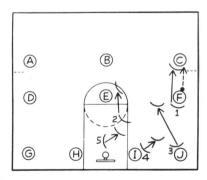

Diagram 51.
Pass: "F"——"C"

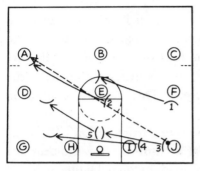

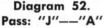

Diagram 52.
Pass: "J"——"A"

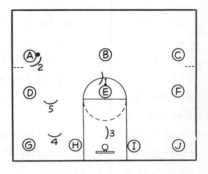

Diagram 53.

the court. Diagram 52 shows the pass from the baseline at "J" to "A."

Diagram 53 shows the defensive alignment when the ball is at "A."

If the ball were to be passed from "A" to "B" and pull #1 "UP" to cover "B," #2 must get back to the top of the circle (as shown in Diagram 54); then if the pass goes from "B" to "C" theoretically #2 should take "C" and #1 drop to the top of the circle as shown in Diagram 55. This situation does not occur very often, but may if a team is stalling or freezing the ball. We have always defended against this type of offense with our 3 out 2 back formation or our defense designed to break up a freeze. Diagram 55 shows the defensive alignment with the ball at "B" and then passed to "C."

The normal defensive alignment when the ball is at "C" is shown in Diagram 51.

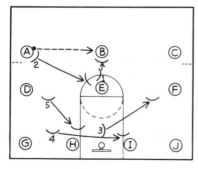

Diagram 54.
Pass: "A"——"B"

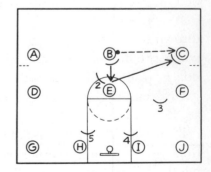

Diagram 55.
Theoretical Position
when Ball is at "B"
and Passed to "C."

TWO OUT—THREE BACK ADJUSTMENTS

We have now explained and shown every defensive slide possible for the basic 2 out 3 back sliding zone. Occasionally we have been forced to make some adjustments from these basic slides; however, this is the basis for the defense. To our knowledge these adjustments have never before been published or seen in print. The only people exposed to these moves have been the players and assistants working directly with us. We are sure that you will find these moves most interesting. They are easy to teach, probably because they have grown out of common sense, therefore making them easy to learn. This is so because they are based upon the premise that the defensive man closest to the man with the ball must cover him.

Perhaps you have noticed in the preceding diagrams explaining the 2 out 3 back moves that the post man "E" has remained in a constant position at the foul line. When the post man moves into a low post or high post just outside of the lane, he presents a different problem for us and as a consequence we have had to deviate from our basic back-line slide.

Diagram 56 illustrates the defensive slides when "E" moves to the side of the foul lane near the ball which is at "F" and #3 is pulled up to guard "F." As "F" passes to "E," #3 turns with the pass and starts his drive for the hoop, but realizes he is screened by "E" and #4 who has to cover "E" in this situation. Therefore, #3 must change his direction and move to the near corner to be ready to cover "J" in case the ball is thrown to "J." Number 5 holds his position in front of the hoop while #1 moves down the sideline to assume his cutoff position in front of "F" and #2 covers the foul line area.

Diagram 57 shows the defensive alignment when the ball is at "E" in the low post position.

Diagram 58 depicts the defensive slides as the ball is passed from "E" to "J" in the corner. When this happens #3 pivots facing the ball as the pass is in flight to the corner. He then moves

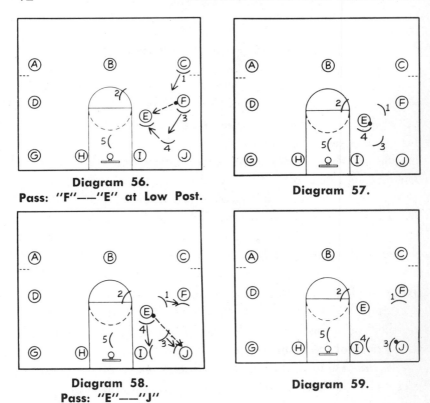

Diagram 56.
Pass: "F"——"E" at Low Post.

Diagram 57.

Diagram 58.
Pass: "E"——"J"

Diagram 59.

to the corner and covers "J." Number 1 moves in front of "F" to the cutoff position along the right sideline, #2 covers the foul line area, #5 holds his position in front of the hoop, and #4 turns with his back to the hoop and faces the ball in the corner.

Diagram 59 illustrates the defensive alignment with the ball located at "J" position.

Another problem confronts us when the offense moves the ball from "F" to "J" to "E" in the low post when #1 is out front and #3 is covering "F." This is shown in Diagram 60.

As the ball is passed to the corner man "J" from "F" and with #3 covering "F," #3 starts his drive toward the hoop and #4 must slide to the corner and cover "J." When #3 gets about halfway in his slide toward the hoop, he must pause at the halfway point while #5 holds his position in front of the hoop,

#2 again protects at the foul line and #1 moves down the sideline toward the cutoff position at "F." These positions are shown in Diagram 61.

Diagram 62 shows the moves when the pass is made from "J" to "E" in the low post. As the pass is executed #3 turns and covers "E." Number 4 then moves to the halfway position, while #1 moves in about one step closer to the ball, leaving #2 to protect the front of the foul circle. Number 5 maintains about the same position in front of the hoop.

Diagram 63 illustrates the defensive alignment with the ball at the "E" position.

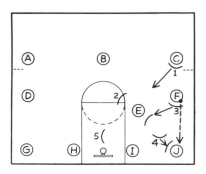

Diagram 60.
Pass: "F"——"J"

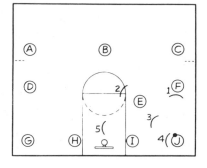

Diagram 61.

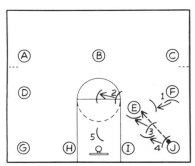

Diagram 62.
Pass: "J"——"E"

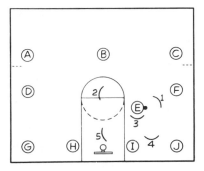

Diagram 63.

Diagram 64 shows the moves when the ball is passed from "E" to "I" along the baseline. Number 5 slides to the baseline and covers "I" while #3 continues on through for the far side of the board and straddles the left lane line facing the ball. Number 4 turns in facing the ball and #2 moves to the left side of the foul line. Number 1 moves to a position along the right side of the foul line with his left hand between "E" and the ball so that he can prevent a pass into "E."

Diagram 65 shows the defensive positions when the ball is at the "I" area.

The moves executed when the ball is passed from "I" to "H" are illustrated in Diagram 66. At this time #3 turns and covers "H" while #5 moves in front of the hoop. Number 4 will move in to the right lane line in front of "I" completing the back-line triangle on the ball. Number 2 moves just outside the foul lane on the left and #1 moves in front of "E" to a position at the foul line with his right foot on the circle's dotted line and his left foot on the right lane line.

Diagram 67 shows the defensive positions when the ball is at "H."

We have diagramed every slide possible for the 2 out 3 back Sliding Zone Defense. Remember, all of these slides are executed the same way on the other side of the court. The only difference is that the moves are made from the left sideline instead of the right. If this defense is to be successful each defensive man must move every time the ball is moved, passed, dribbled, or shot. The players performing this defense must be properly motivated, must be willing to work hard, hustle at all times, and keep alert and be aggressive. As we have mentioned before, this is strictly a team defense which requires the utmost in teamwork and cooperation.

We have been asked many times for the secret of our defense. If there is one secret, we would have to say it is work! Work hard on perfecting the slides which have been illustrated.

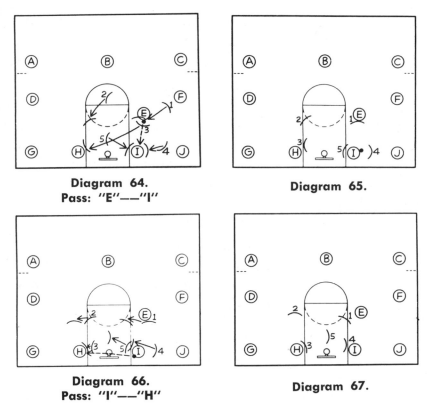

Diagram 64.
Pass: "E"——"I"

Diagram 65.

Diagram 66.
Pass: "I"——"H"

Diagram 67.

One of the best ways we have found for perfecting these slides is by getting the players to become so familiar with the slides that it is no problem for them to play any position. For instance, the front-line positions are interchangeable as are the back-line positions. We do not expect the back-line players to exchange with the front line. In our years of experience we have tried converting back-line men to front-line positions and vice-versa. It is a great attribute in a man to be able to play both front and back on defense; we have found this type of player to be very rare.

This team defense must be practiced daily so its effectiveness will be maintained. The following are the front-line drills and the back-line drills which we use. While using these drills we constantly stress the individual fundamentals of basketball, footwork, pivots, and quickness of hand movement.

FRONT-LINE DRILL

In this drill we use 8 offensive men against 2 defensive men. The object is to teach the defensive men their slides so they can get to the cutoff positions (at the post and along the sides) where they will be in a position to intercept the ball when it comes into these areas.

Rules to be observed for this drill are:

1. The 8 offensive men are not all allowed to move.
2. Neither corner man ("G" or "J") is allowed to shoot the ball, they are strictly passers. All other men are allowed to shoot if they have time.
3. The offensive man located in the "E" area may pass out front to "A," "B," or "C" only. He is not permitted to pass to "D" or "F" because they would be picked up by a backline man.
4. We work various combinations of players in the two defensive positions. After they have worked awhile we then move them to an offensive position for a little rest and drill two more men.

All of our drills are parts taken from the basic defense. As you study and use these drills you will notice a close resemblance to the basic basketball fundamentals we discussed in Chapter 2; one-on-one, two-on-two, three-on-two, and three-on-three.

Diagram 68 shows the slides when #1 is "UP" and the ball is passed from "B" to "A." Number 2 moves out to cover "A" while #1 drops to the top of the foul circle and tries to prevent a direct pass into the post from "A."

Diagram 69 illustrates the moves when the ball is passed

from "E" to "B" out front. Number 1 must shuttle right along with the ball and cover "B" while #2 continues on back to the top of the foul circle toward "E."

"E" cannot pass inside to "D," "G," "F" or "J" because they are the responsibility of the back line. He is permitted to pass back out to "A," "B" or "C." If "E" passes to "C," number 1 must go after "C" and #2 drop back on "E" at the post as shown in Diagram 70.

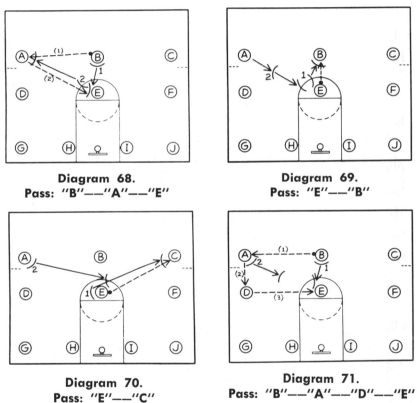

Diagram 68.
Pass: "B"——"A"——"E"

Diagram 69.
Pass: "E"——"B"

Diagram 70.
Pass: "E"——"C"

Diagram 71.
Pass: "B"——"A"——"D"——"E"

This part of the front-line drill is very similar to the three-against-two drill. It is hard work and the defense at first will fall behind; but as the drill is continued and the defensive men learn to move with the ball, they will be able to make all of the defensive slides with a much higher degree of success.

When the pass is made from "B" to "A" to "D" to "E" in the post, the front-line men are not responsible for covering "D" on the side. This is a back-line man's responsibility and is covered in the back-line drills. The front line is responsible for the coverage on "E" at the post, and if the man responsible for covering "E" can, he should try to intercept the pass from "D" to "E." The slides for this part of the drill are illustrated in Diagram 71.

As illustrated in the diagram, #1 drops back to the foul circle at "E" trying to intercept the pass from "D." Number 2 is shown on his way back.

The front line is also responsible for executing the cutoff play along the sideline. The drill for executing the cutoff play has two possibilities. The first is when #1 is "UP" covering "B" who has the ball, and #2 is back and off to the side of the key. As the ball is passed from "B" to "D," #2 will slide to his left and pick up "D" as shown in Diagram 72.

As the pass is made from "D" to "G" in the corner (remember "G" will be covered by a back-line man) #2 will simply turn facing "G" in the corner and play between "D" and "G" looking for the pass back out to "D" as shown in Diagram 73. If #2 intercepts the ball as it is thrown out he has successfully executed the cutoff play. Number 1 positions as shown at the foul line.

The second possibility for executing the cutoff play occurs when #2 is "UP." Diagram 74 shows #2 in the "UP" position covering "B" who has the ball. Number 1 is in the back position.

You must remember when the ball is at "B" with #2 "UP," "D" will be covered by a back-line man. As the ball is passed from "B" to "D," #2 drops to the left side of the foul line as shown in Diagram 75. Number 1 turns toward the ball and takes a position at the foul line as shown.

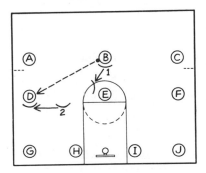

Diagram 72.
Pass: "B"——"D"

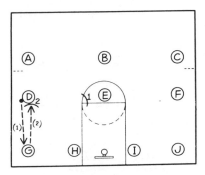

Diagram 73.
Pass: "D"——"G"——"D"

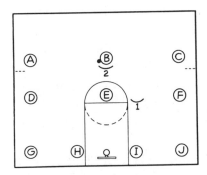

Diagram 74.
Ball at "B" #2 in "UP" Position

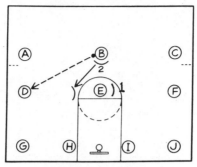

Diagram 75.
Pass: "B"——"D"

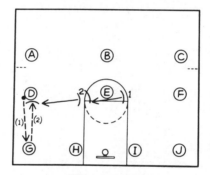

Diagram 76.
Pass: "D"——"G"——"D"

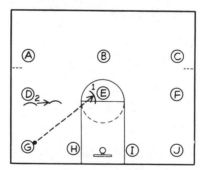

Diagram 77.
Pass: "G"——"E"

As the ball is passed from "D" to "G" (as shown in Diagram 76), #2 slides to the cutoff position between "D" and "G" who has the ball in the corner.

It is now apparent that #2 and #1 are in the same positions as previously illustrated in Diagram 73 and in position to make the cutoff play. The final move of this drill is very simple. If "G" passes to "E" in the post, #1 tries to intercept at "E" and #2 moves halfway between the foul lane and the sideline as shown in Diagram 77.

BACK-LINE DRILL

The purpose of this drill is to train the back-line men to move so they can defend the wings and corners, and slide to protect the middle area in front of the hoop. It also teaches the back-line men how to interchange all three positions and become adept at playing any back-line position.

Eight men against three. In this drill we use 8 offensive men against three defensive men. The rules to remember for this drill are:

1. The offensive men are not allowed to move from their position. They must hold with or without the ball.
2. Offensive man "B" is a ball handler, see Diagram 78. He may dribble from right to left with not more than two bounces. This will help in determining which back-line man is "UP." You must assume that "B" is covered by the front-line man on the right or left of center. Thus, this will bring the back-line man on that side "UP." Offensive player "B" may not shoot, but he is allowed to pass to any of the other 7 offensive players.
3. Any time the ball goes to the men along the baseline ("G," "H," "I" or "J") and they pass out to "B," "D" or "F," the play is "dead," because these men would be picked up by the front-line men.

4. The baseline men may pass to the post man, and he is permitted to pass inside or to the corners. If he is not covered he may shoot. It is a back-line responsibility to stop the post man from shooting.

Diagram 78 shows the basic setup for the back-line drill with "B" moving from side to side and pulling #3 to the "UP" position.

From this basic position we are concerned about covering the side, corner, post and underneath. There are 5 plays we are concerned with: (1) front–side–corner—"B"–"F"–"J"; (2) front–side–post–under hoop on left side of the lane—"B"–"F"–"E"–"H"; (3) front–direct to corner—"B"–"J"; (4) front–side–corner–near side under hoop–far side under hoop—"B"–"F"–"J"–"I"–"H" (5) front–post man–under hoop or to corner—"B"–"E"–"I"/"H"/"J"/"G." Diagram 79 illustrates play #1–front–side–corner.

When the ball is passed to "F," #3 slides over and covers "F" (see Diagram 79). Number 4 also starts his move to the half-way position between the corner and the center of the foul line (designated by arrow on #4's path). Number 5 moves to a position in front of the hoop and holds, facing the ball, and #3 starts his drive for the hoop as the ball is passed from "F" to "J." Number 4 continues to the corner and covers "J."

Diagram 80 illustrates play #2–front–side–post–under the hoop on left side of the lane.

As the ball is passed from "F" to "E," #3 slides under the hoop to a position along the right lane line. Number 5 slides up and covers "E" at the post and #4 slides from his halfway position to the far side of the lane where he covers "H." This move may seem difficult, but it can be made very effective if #4 moves as the pass leaves "F." Many times #4 will be there in time to intercept the pass from "E" to "H."

Diagram 81 illustrates play #3–front–direct to the corner. When the ball is passed from "B" to "J," #3, if he is playing his position correctly with his hands up, will force the pass to be high. This will give #4 enough time to get to the corner and cover "J." Often, #4 will get there in time to deflect or intercept the ball. Number 3 drives back toward the hoop for a position in front of "I" and between him and the ball in the corner. Number 5 holds his position in front of the hoop.

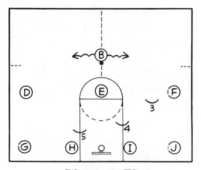

Diagram 78.
Starting Position—Back-Line Drill

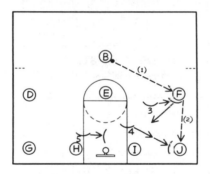

Diagram 79.
Pass: "B"——"F"——"J"

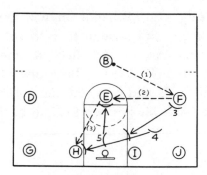

Diagram 80.
Pass: "B"——"F"——"E"——"H"

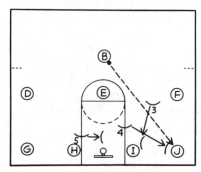

Diagram 81.
Pass: "B"——"J"

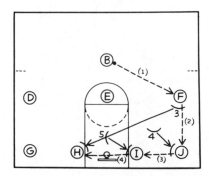

Diagram 82.
Pass: "B"——"F"——"J"——"I"——"H"

Diagram 82 illustrates play #4—front—side—corner—near side under hoop—far side under hoop.

With #3 covering "F" on the side, #4 is at the halfway position, with #5 holding in front of the hoop. Then the remaining passes of the series are completed. The action is as follows: #4 covers "J" in the corner, #3 starts his drive to the far side of the hoop (this slide is the longest slide in all of these situations and it takes exactly seven steps or running strides by an average size player; all other slides can be completed in three strides or less), #5 must move to the baseline and cover "I" while #3 continues on through and picks up "H" at the far side of the lane. Number 3 coming through gets a beautiful chance to discourage "H" from shooting because he will arrive at "H" about the same time the ball does. If "H" passes to "G," #3 will continue to the corner, #5 will take the middle in front of "H" and #4 who has left the corner will come in front of the hoop and hold. They will end up in the positions shown in Diagram 83.

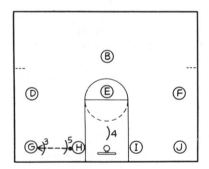

Diagram 83.
Pass: "H"——"G" and Defensive
Positions with Ball at "G"

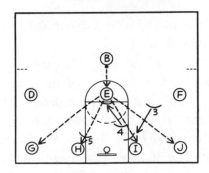

Diagram 84.
Pass: "B"——"E"——"I"/"H"/"J"/"G"

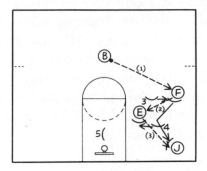

Diagram 85.
Pass: "B"——"F"——"E"——"J"

Diagram 84 illustrates play #5—front—post man—under the hoop or to the corner.

When the ball comes directly into the post man "E," #4 must slide up and cover the post, #5 holds, and #3 moves toward the hoop to a position in front of "I" facing the ball at "E." Any pass from "E" to "I" or "J" must be covered by #3. Number 4 will drop straight back toward the hoop. If the ball is passed from "E" to "H" or "G" on the other side of the court, #5 must cover and #4 will drop back toward the hoop facing the ball.

Low Post Drill. The low post drill for the back line involves two plays. Play #1 is from the front to side, into the low post, to the corner: "B"–"F"–"E"–"J." Play #2 is from the front, to the side, into the corner, then to the low post: "B"–"F"–"J"–"E." This drill involves only 4 offensive men against 3 defensive men.

Diagram 85 illustrates low post play #1.

With "E" in the low post and outside of the lane, and the ball passed from "B" to "F," #3 must cover "F," and as the pass is made from "F" to "E," #4 slides with the pass and covers "E." Number 3 starts back and as the pass is made from "E" to "J" #3 just pivots and turns toward "J" in the corner. Number 5 holds his position in front of the hoop.

Diagram 86 illustrates low post play #2.

When the ball is passed from "B" to "F" #3 must cover "F," and as the pass is made to "J" in the corner, #4 slides from the halfway position and covers "J." Number 3 starts his drive toward the hoop and when he reaches a point between "J" and "E," #3 pauses. As the pass is made to "E," #3 pivots and covers "E" and #5 continues to hold in front of the hoop.

This is the complete set of front- and back-line slides and drills for the two out–three back Sliding Zone Defense. The drills are parts of the two out–three back defense; they are the important plays which the defense must execute. The coach and the players must have knowledge of the previously dis-

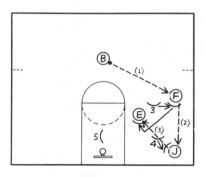

Diagram 86.
Pass: "B"——"F"——"J"——"E"

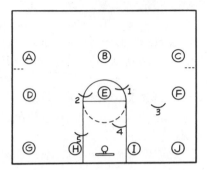

Diagram 87.
Ten Against Five Setup.

cussed fundamentals of basketball, one-on-one, two-on-one, two-on-two, three-on-two, three-on-three. These situations are prevalent throughout this defense. Learn these fundamentals so you can recognize them in the various play situations. Start out with these drills at a slow pace so as to facilitate the defensive players' learning their moves and becoming more skilled in the execution of these moves. Then and only then allow the offensive players to speed up the movement of the ball until they reach top speed.

TEN AGAINST FIVE DRILL

When you feel the defensive players have acquired some skill at making their slides, you may use the ten against five drill and move the ball to any and all of the offensive positions. At first, don't permit the offense to shoot the ball. After the drill has been run for five or ten minutes then permit the offense to shoot if they are not covered. If a man is open and gets an easy shot, stop the drill, retrace the passes leading up to the shot, check the sliding assignment until you find who is making the mistake, then correct it. Repetition, that is, patience, is a virtue in teaching this defense. There are other ways to expedite learning—awarding points for interceptions, deflected passes, harassed shots, and in general rewarding good defensive plays.

It is difficult for five men to stop ten from scoring. This drill has been very helpful in aiding our defensive work by teaching cooperation and teamwork. Five men working intelligently, enthusiastically, and with desire can make it very difficult for ten men to get a good shot.

Diagram 87 shows the setup for ten against five. It is the same as in the diagrams we have been using to illustrate all of the slides.

A QUIZ TO TEST YOUR DEFENSIVE KNOW-HOW

Here is a game we have devised to test your knowledge of the defense. The questions will be from the offensive standpoint, the letters are the passes and the defensive numbers are the answers. The correct number should correspond with the letter receiving the pass. Every move on the two out–three back will be covered.

PASS (Question)

1. "B"——"F"——"J"   1. 1, 3, 4   (Example)
2. "B"——"F"——"J"——"I"
3. "B"——"F"——"J"——"I"
4. ——"H"——"G"
5. "C"——"F"——"E"——"H"
6. "B"——"E"——"G"/"H"
7. "C"——"F"——"J"——"F"
8. ——"C"
9. "J"——"A"
10. "A"——"B"——"C"

LOW POST PLAYS

11. "C"——"F"——"E"——"J"
12. "C"——"F"——"J"——"E"
13. ——"I"——"H"

This has been Quiz 1. There are two more quizzes at the end of later chapters. Answers on page 210.

4

Three Out—Two Back Sliding Zone

The 3 out 2 back sliding zone defense is designed to defend against outside shooting, to force a pass inside near the basket, and then slide, shifting the defensive strength closer to the basket area. This is our active defense, or attack zone, from which we derive all of our pressing tactics which will be covered in following chapters.

The most important factor to remember in teaching zone defense is: each time the offensive team moves the ball (dribbles or passes) all five defensive men must automatically slide to a position on the court relative to the position of the ball and the basket area.

SELECTION OF PERSONNEL

The selection of personnel to fit into the various positions of this defense is of the utmost importance. We have found that players possessing the following qualities have been most successful:

1. Can be a small man—very active (lot of energy)
2. Ideal to have fairly tall, rangy man—long arms and quick hands
3. He is key to fast break
4. Should be excellent ball handler and passer
5. Should be good with either hand
6. Should be very good dribbler
7. Should be able to cut off pass to front half of foul circle

1. Should be fairly tall and rugged
2. Agile enough to move well
3. Should be able to shoot driving in from left to facilitate fast break
4. Should be a good ball handler to help fast break
5. Should be able to rebound on the move
6. A shorter stronger player can play this position if he is tough enough to get the inside rebound position
7. Must defend against good shooters here and in corner

1. Same as Number 2
2. Should be able to shoot driving from right

1. Second largest or tallest player
2. Much the same qualities as Number 5
3. Must be able to defend against the post man

1. Biggest and strongest man on the team
2. Rugged and hard working
3. Able to rebound while moving
4. Able to rebound from standing position
5. Must be a good passer with one-hand pass or long pass to get fast break started
6. Must be able to move and cover corner

BASIC THREE OUT–TWO BACK SLIDES

Starting Positions. The following diagrams illustrate the basic slides of the five men employing the 3 out 2 back sliding zone defense. There are two starting positions for the back-line men (#4 and #5). These positions are the key to this defense and they must be assumed quickly and properly in order that the defensive strength will be balanced toward the ball, from where the offensive attack will come. One position is called the "UP" position, the other is the "Back" position. These positions are determined by the location of the ball when it is out front and on the left side of the court. The left back-line man (#4) is in the "UP" position and the right back-line man (#5) is in the "BACK" position. (Note: the middle of the court is shown by a broken line.)

The exact position of #4 is with his left foot on the left lane line and his right foot touching the broken line of the foul circle. Number 5 takes his position about three feet in front of the hoop and a little to the right with his right foot touching the right lane line, as shown in Diagram 88.

If the ball is on the right side of the court, the positions are reversed with #5 moving to the "UP" position on the right side of the lane and #4 dropping straight back on the left side and assuming the "BACK" position at this point (see Diagram 89).

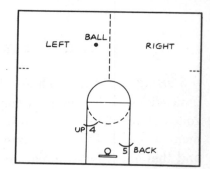

Diagram 88.

Photo 10. This illustrates the 3 out 2 back Sliding Zone, starting positions—back-line man #50 in the "UP" position, back-line man #52 in the "BACK" position. This photo corresponds to Diagram 88.

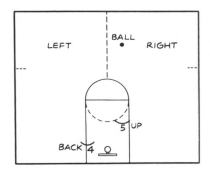

Diagram 89.

Photo 11.   This photograph illustrates the 3 out 2 back Sliding Zone, starting positions—back-line man #52 in the "UP" position, back-line man #50 in the "BACK" position. This photo corresponds to Diagram 89.

Sliding Method. These positions may also be assumed by another method we refer to as the sliding method (see Diagram 90). This is done by having #4, when he is in the "UP" position on the left, just slide to his right and take the "UP" position on the right. At the same time #5 slides to his left and takes the left "BACK" position.

When the offense brings the ball directly down the center of the court on the imaginary dotted line, the back-line men must decide which one will assume the "UP" position. This is usually decided by the style of play being employed by the offensive team. As the game progresses the offensive team will establish its play pattern to one side of the court or the other. Depending upon the offensive pattern being employed or by the habits of the offensive players, you can usually predetermine which side of the court a team is likely to use. Good scouting reports will provide this information.

Remember, when employing the 3 out 2 back zone it is absolutely imperative to have your back line deployed in the exact positions explained in Diagrams 88, 89, and 90. The defense will not give the desired coverage if the back-line men are not able to move automatically to the "UP" and "BACK" positions. We have explained both methods of securing the back-line positions. They both have proved to be satisfactory. We would suggest that you try each and then use the one better suited for your personnel.

Where a coach decides to position the front line is dependent on how well the opposing team shoots from the outside. That is, the front line should set up their defense farther out when playing against good long-range shooters. This rule of thumb definitely applies to coaching college basketball and it is probably quite appropriate to use in coaching high school basketball. Many high school players are exceptionally accurate from 20 to 25 feet away.

Defensive Coverage of All Possible Passing Plays. The fol-

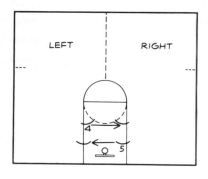

Diagram 90.

lowing diagrams and explanations depict the defensive positions and moves of the five men employing the 3 out 2 back sliding zone, when the ball is moved to different positions by the offensive team.

Diagram 91 shows the starting position of the 3 out 2 back zone when the ball is in the area of #1 at "B." The main job of #1 is to keep the ball out of the foul circle area. He usually doesn't move too far from the circle unless he has to stop the long shooting of "B" or if the defense is employing the half-court press. Number 2 places his right foot about a half step from the foul line where it intersects the circle, while #3

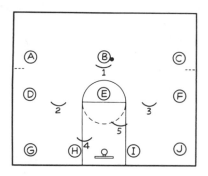

Diagram 91.

places his left foot at the same position at the opposite side of the foul line. The two back men, numbers 4 and 5, take their positions "UP" and "BACK" as previously described in Diagrams 88, 89, and 90 with #5 taking the "UP" position and #4 the "BACK" position. These two men must talk to each other, the "UP" man calling "UP" and the "BACK" man calling "BACK."

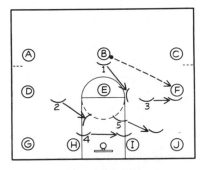

Diagram 92.
Pass: "B"——"F"

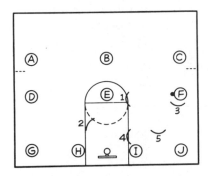

Diagram 93.
Ball at "F"

Diagram 92 illustrates the slides when the ball is passed from "B" to "F," or from the center-front to the side.

In this particular series, #3 slides over and covers "F," #1 slides to a position at the right side of the foul line between "E" and "F" while #5 moves to the halfway position between the center of the foul line and the right corner of the court. Number 4 moves to a position on the right lane line and #2 slides to a position with his left foot on the dotted line and his right foot on the left lane line as shown in Diagram 92.

Diagram 93 shows the defensive positions when the ball is at "F," and Diagram 94 shows the slides when the ball is passed from "F" to "J" in the corner.

As shown in the diagram, #3 turns with the pass and faces "J" in the corner looking for the cutoff in case "J" passes back to "F." Number 5 slides to the corner and covers "J," while #4 moves halfway to the corner near the baseline. Number 2 moves to a position directly in front of the hoop and faces the corner, and #1 turns facing the corner and holds his position at the right side of the foul line preventing a pass from "J" to "E." Diagram 95 shows defensive positions when the ball is at "J."

At this point we actually have a 2 out 3 back alignment. If the offense moves into a low post attack by moving "E" into a low post, we use the same coverage as demonstrated by our 2 out 3 back defense in Chapter 3. If we are fortunate enough to have #3 cover "F," this allows our back line to move very little, giving us a much stronger defense. You will notice how much more difficult the slides become when #3 has to cover "C" and #5 has to come out and cover "F" as illustrated in the following series of diagrams.

Diagram 96 illustrates the defensive slides when the ball is passed from "B" to "C." Number 3 moves into guarding position between the ball handler "C" and the basket. Number 1 takes a position on the foul circle between the ball handler and

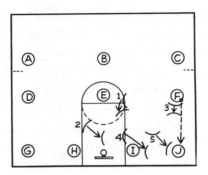

Diagram 94.
Pass: "F"——"J"

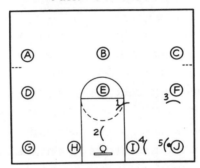

Diagram 95.
Ball at "J"

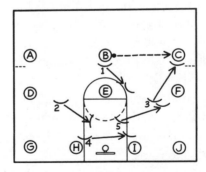

Diagram 96.
Pass: "B"——"C"

the foul line. Back-line man #5 sets up about a half step behind the foul line extended, halfway between the right side of the foul circle and the right sideline. The other back-line man (#4) takes a position with his left foot on one side of the right lane line and his right foot on the other side, straddling the right lane line. Number 2 moves to his right about one step along the broken line of the foul circle. All the men must end up facing the ball handler as illustrated in Diagram 97.

Diagram 98 indicates the slides and the positions of the defensive men after the ball has been passed from "C" to "F," or from the front to the side.

Back-line man #5 takes a guarding position between the ball handler "F" and the basket. Defensive front-line man #3 turns facing the ball and moves about one step closer to the ball. Number 1 deploys on the side of the foul circle between the ball handler and the foul line, his main job being to keep the ball out of the foul circle area. The other back-line man (#4) sets up near the mid-point of an imaginary line between the corner and the center of the foul line. Number 2 takes a position in front of the basket with his left foot on the dotted line. It is imperative that all of the defensive men face the ball handler "F."

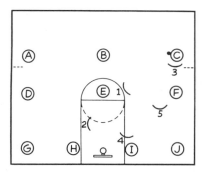

Diagram 97.

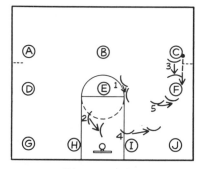

Diagram 98.
Pass: "C"——"F"

Diagram 99 depicts the movements of the men as the ball is passed from "F" to "J" in the corner. As "F" passes the ball, #4 moves to the corner and covers "J." Number 5 turns facing the ball and drives for a position under the hoop, while #2 holds his position in front of the hoop until #5 approaches and then releases his position and slides to a position at the junction of the foul line and foul circle. Number 1 turns and faces the corner while #3 drops toward the side at "F" and takes a position facing the offensive man "J" with the ball in the corner and tries to intercept any pass which may come out along the sideline.

After this movement is completed the positions of all five defensive men should be as shown in Diagram 100.

If "J" passes to "I," #5 will take "I" as the pass is executed and #2 will move into a position nearer the hoop. Number 4 will move with the ball to a position under the hoop, bypassing #5 as he passes "I" and taking a "whack" at the ball. We call this looping. As #4 goes by #5 and approaches his position in

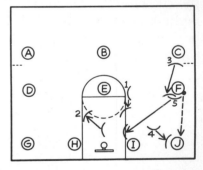

Diagram 99.
Pass: "F"——"J"

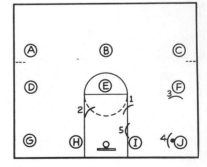

Diagram 100.

front of the hoop, #2 will return to his position at the foul line. If "I" passes back to "J," #5 must go with the pass and take "J" in the corner. Diagram 101 illustrates this move. It may appear that this maneuver is impossible; however, the contrary is true—with a little practice. This maneuver can be excellently executed and is one of the most effective moves in this defense.

Diagram 102 shows the slides which must be executed when the ball is thrown out front to "B" from the corner man "J." Note that the defensive positions are the same as they were in Diagram 91 with one exception: #4 is now in the "UP" position and #5 is in the "BACK" position. The reason for this is that they are the closest men to these positions in this particular play. These positions are illustrated in Diagram 103.

Diagram 104 indicates the slides when the ball is passed into the high post or foul line area to "E" from "B." The backline man #4, who is the "UP" man, moves into a defensive position between "E" and the basket while the other back-

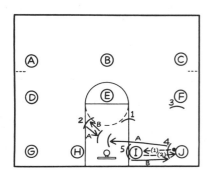

Diagram 101.
Pass: "J"——"I"——"J"

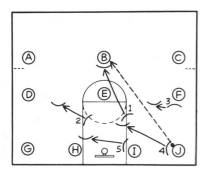

Diagram 102.
Pass: "J"——"B"

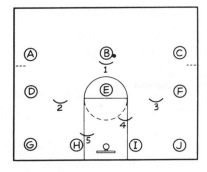

Diagram 103.
Ball at "B"

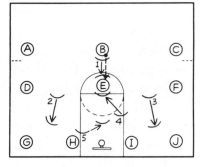

Diagram 104.
Pass: "B"——"E"

line man moves into a position between the lane lines directly in front of the hoop.

Defensive front-line men #2 and #3 drop back to a position halfway between the corner and the center of the foul line, forming a cup around the ball handler "E." Simultaneously, #1 turns and drops back on the ball handler and double-teams along with #4. Again all defensive men are facing the ball as shown in Diagram 105.

From this defensive alignment, #2 and #3 have the initial responsibility of cutting off a pass to "G" or "J" in the corners. If the ball gets into the corner, they must cover the man with the ball in their particular corner. If the ball is passed from the corner man "J" to "F," #3 must go with the pass and pick up "F." It is the same on the other side: if "G" passes to "D," defensive man #2 must go along with the pass and pick up "D."

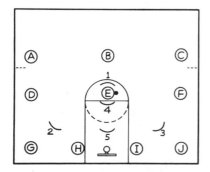

Diagram 105.

Photo 12. This photograph illustrates the 3 out 2 back Sliding Zone positions when the ball is at post in the middle. Wing men #34 and #44 are in positions halfway between the corner and center of the foul line. This photo corresponds to Diagram 105.

If "E" passes inside to "H" or "I," back-line man #5 must take the first pass and back-line man #4 must pick up the other man. To explain this move another way, it is the 3 on 2 principle working. If "E" passes to "H," #5 will take "H" and #4 will drop straight back and cover "I." In the meantime, #1 will slip around "E" toward the ball to prevent a return pass from "H" to "E." (See Diagram 106.)

Remember, all of these slides are executed the same way on the other side of the court. Every defensive man must move with every pass, he must keep his eyes on the ball at all times. He must hustle all the time, and he must be alert and aggressive. This is a team defense, players must help one another and work together, and promote teamwork by talking (intelligently). Such voice signals as "I'm UP" or "I'm Back," "I've got this man," "you take him," "I've got this side, you take the middle" are all intelligent phrases which aid better teamwork.

This is a team defense and it must be practiced daily in order to keep it effective. The following are some of the drills we use to help maintain its effectiveness and facilitate learning. Throughout the use of these drills, we stress facing the ball at all times, keeping the hands up, and knees slightly bent to facilitate quick movement—stressing at all times moving with the ball whether it is passed or dribbled and never turning your back on the ball.

FRONT-LINE DRILLS

Six Men Against Three: The purpose of this drill is to train the defensive men to move with the ball and prevent a shot from out front, on the side, and in the corner when the pass comes from "E" at the foul circle.

Rules for This Drill: (1) offensive men must hold their positions and move the ball; (2) offensive man "E" cannot shoot the ball (because he would be covered by a back-line man).

1. When the ball is at "E" defensive men #2 and #3 must take the position halfway between the corner and center of the foul line (see Diagram 107). From this position #2 and #3 can slide to the corners or the side as shown in Diagrams 108 and 109. Number 1 moves around and in front of "E" on the side toward the ball.

2. The rule here is that the side men "F" and "D" may only pass to "B," "E," or in this case "F" to "D." If they pass to

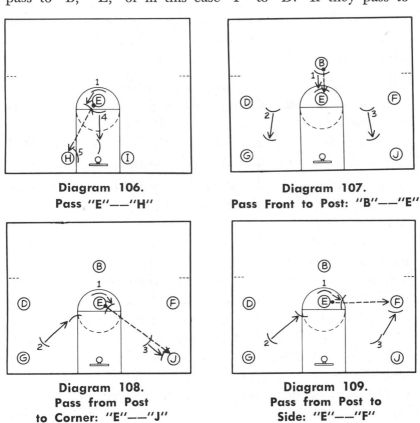

Diagram 106.
Pass "E"——"H"

Diagram 107.
Pass Front to Post: "B"——"E"

Diagram 108.
Pass from Post
to Corner: "E"——"J"

Diagram 109.
Pass from Post to
Side: "E"——"F"

"G" or "J" from here, the play is "dead" and the drill is started over. The reason for "killing" the play when the side men pass to the corner is that these corner men will be covered by the back-line men. (See Back-Line Drills, below.)

3. When the ball is in the corner and passed to the side from "J" to "F" defensive man #3 moves with the pass to cover "F" on the side (Diagram 110). Remember, these moves are the same on the other side of the court.

BACK-LINE DRILLS

Here we have 8 men against 2. This seems like an impossible situation unless you have rules governing the offensive men. Rules to remember for this drill are:

1. Offensive man "B" is just a ball handler
2. Offensive man "E" may shoot, but is limited in that he may only pass to offensive men "H" and "I"
3. Once the ball is passed to "G," "H," "I" or "J" they cannot pass back out; if they do, it kills the play

Diagram 111 shows the slide when #4 is in the "UP" position and the ball is passed from "B" to "E."

In Diagram 112 you see the slide when the ball is passed from "E" to "H," defensive man #5 taking "H" and #4 dropping back toward the hoop to cut off a pass to "I."

Diagram 113 illustrates the moves when the ball is passed from "H" to "G." Defensive man #5 slides to the corner and covers "G" while defensive man #4 slides around and in front of "H" trying to keep the ball away from "H." Diagrams 111, 112, and 113 indicate the defensive slides against the inside attack.

The following diagrams will show the moves against the side-line attack. In Diagram 114 we must assume that "B" has pulled the front-line man up and back-line man #4 moves up to the foul line extended so he is in position to cover "F."

With #4 covering "F," back-line man #5 takes a position halfway between the corner and the center of the foul line.

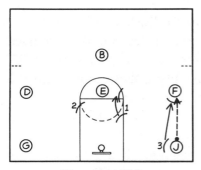

Diagram 110.
Pass from Corner to
Side: "J"——"F"

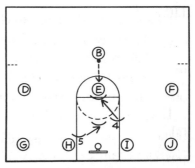

Diagram 111.
Pass from Front to
Post: "B"——"E"

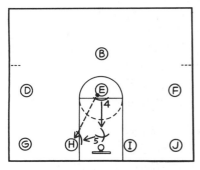

Diagram 112.
Pass from Post to Inside
Lane Position: "E"——"H"

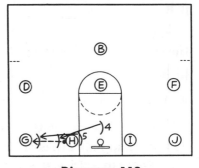

Diagram 113.
Pass from Inside Lane Man
to Corner: "H"——"G"

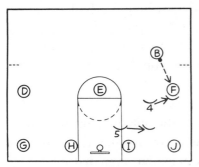

Diagram 114.
Pass from Front to
Side: "B"——"F"

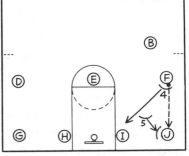

Diagram 115.
Pass from Side to
Corner: "F"——"J"

Diagram 115 depicts the slide as the ball is passed from "F" to "J" in the corner. Number 4 drives for the hoop as #5 takes "J" in the corner.

Diagram 116 shows the slide as "J" passes to "I." Number 4 takes "I" and #5 drives from the corner to the hoop and is in position to cover "H" or take "I" if "I" should pass back to corner "J," in which case #4 will slide to the corner taking "J." Here you have the looping technique being employed as it was previously explained in connection with Diagram 101.

This is the complete set of back-line and front-line drills for the three out–two back zone. Observe the rules and remember to have your offensive men move the ball slowly at first, and as the defensive men become more familiar with the slides increase the speed of the movement of the ball until it is moved as fast as possible.

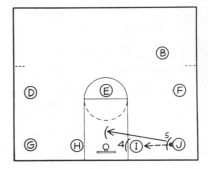

Diagram 116.
Pass from Corner to
Inside Lane Man: "J"——"I"

TEN AGAINST FIVE DRILL

After the defense has acquired some skill at making the slides, we then use ten offensive men against five defensive men. It is understood that five men cannot guard ten men on an individual basis, but this encourages the five defensive men to cooperate with each other and work as a team. Again, do not permit the offensive men to leave their designated positions. They are permitted to shoot when they are open.

While executing this drill we stress the use of proper foot and hand movements related to fundamental defensive play. We constantly remind the defensive players to use near-arm guarding and windmilling techniques when they are involved in one-on-one, two-on-one, two-on-two or three-on-two situations.

AREA COVERAGE

The area which a defensive player must protect will vary according to several factors. We believe it is foolish to establish a list of specific hard and fast "rules" with respect to floor or area responsibilities. Instead, the area a player covers will depend on:

1. The size of the opponent playing opposite him
2. The speed of the opponent
3. The ability of the opponents in nearby zone areas
4. Factors such as score, tempo, and time of the game.

These factors not only determine the size of the area to be covered, but also how far forward, back, left or right a front-line man must play to help a back-line player, or vice versa.

TOUCH-OFF TECHNIQUE

The touch-off is simply a signal from one defensive man to another. A defensive player uses the touch-off to indicate that he is ready to pick up the offensive player with the ball who is about to enter his area. The signal is an actual touching of a teammate as if to say: "The man with the ball is now in my zone—I'll take him!" We also accompany this move with voice signals whenever practicable. In Diagram 117, as #1 and "B" approach the adjacent area, #2 moves to pick up "B" who is being covered by #1. Employing the near-arm guarding

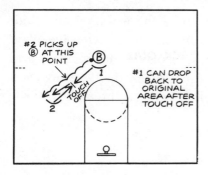

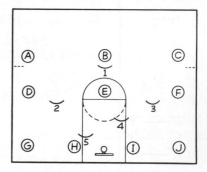

Diagram 117.
Touch-off and Pickup by #2

Diagram 118.

technique, #1 has his right hip in and right arm up. The left hand will be lowered trying to deflect the dribble. At the same time the left arm and hand act as a feeler ready to receive the touch off signal from #2. In this situation #2 will use his right hand to touch #1's left hand. This will release #1 enabling him to return to his middle area of responsibility. Defensive player #2 picks up the dribbler and covers him one-on-one. This technique is similar to the man-for-man defensive switching fundamental. It is employed in all directions in all of our zone formations, front to back, right to left, left to right, back to front and diagonally.

Diagram 118 illustrates the 3 out 2 back - 10 against 5 drill setup.

Here is a game you can play to test yourself as to which defensive man should cover the offensive man with the ball.

THREE OUT–TWO BACK QUIZ

PASS (Question)

1. "B"——"F"——"J"   1. 1, 3, 4 (Example)
2. "C"——"F"——"J"
3. "A"——"G"——"D"
4. "C"——"F"——"E"——"I"
5. "B"——"E"——"H"
6. "A"——"E"——"H"
7. "B"——"A"——"G"——"E"
8. "C"——"F"——"E"——"H"

This is Quiz 2. Answers on page 210.

5

Two-One-Two
Sliding Zone or Four Man Zone

We have often been asked to give the "secret" of the Sliding Zone Defense. Our answer to this has been a stock one: work intelligently. If there really is any secret, we would have to say it is our 2-1-2 defense. To the author's knowledge, nothing has been written or published regarding this defense. It has been most successful in every game in which we have used it. We have never used it for an entire game, usually only for five or ten minutes a half. We have found that without fail this defense would check our opponents, holding them to perhaps one or two field goals for a five or ten minute period and often shutting them out completely. This would allow us to overtake our opponents or widen our lead and control the remainder of the game. During the time this defense was applied, our opponents would become concerned and usually try to change their offense. More often than not we could outscore them after they changed their offense, and once we had a lead, we would revert to one of our basic zones.

FOUR MEN ON HALF COURT

Our 2-1-2 or four man Sliding Zone came about during practice sessions. We were working on front-line and back-line
drills when we observed that the back-line drill for the 3 out 2
back zone and the 2 out drill for the 2 out 3 back zone when
pulled together would result in half-court coverage with 4 men:
2 out and 2 back employing the moves of each defense. For
example, we use 4 men against 10, as explained in Diagram
119 which shows the basic setup of 4 against 10.

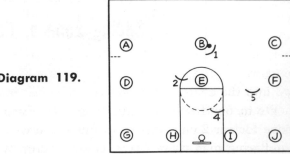

Diagram 119.

With the ball at "B" on the right side of the court, #1 and
#5 are in the "UP" positions. When the ball is moved, #1 and
#2 play exactly the same moves of the 2 out 3 back defense
explained in Chapter 3. Numbers 4 and 5 play exactly as they
do in Chapter 4, 3 out 2 back. Their back-line moves are exactly the same. Incorporating these moves gives a pretty good
four man zone coverage. True, it is most difficult and practically
impossible for 4 men to cover 10; however, it is excellent as
a drill. The four men can keep up pretty well, for from 3 to 6
minutes, then it becomes too much of a physical impossibility
because it takes a lot of energy for four men to cover the entire
defensive half of the court.

Middle Man on Post. Now by applying these principles and
inserting our fifth man, #3, into the defense, it gives our de-

fense more manpower, and maneuverability. We can use #3 to play their post man, man-for-man, wherever he goes, or we can play him in a zone position, in the foul circle area. If we use him man-for-man, the back line must play our standard moves and cover the post. Our front line must do likewise, cutting the ball off to the post and using the cutoff play at the sideline on the pass from the corner back out along the sideline.

Middle Man in Foul Circle. If we use #3 as a zone player in the foul circle, we have a rule which limits his movement. He is allowed to go anywhere in or around the circle as long as he keeps one foot on the line of the circle. This will permit him to play with one foot outside of the circle, thus giving him a pretty good range and a lot of area in the middle to cover. This also gives us the name for this defense—2-1-2. The man in the middle is thus referred to as "1," but his number remains "3" for the purpose of diagraming. When we insert #3 into the center for zone play, we must make a few adjustments to our front line and back line. First, we must add a move for our 2 out front men. The move we add is a modified 3 out wing man move which brings #2 under the hoop when the ball is passed down the right side and into the corner at "J." Diagrams 120 and 121 show this move.

Diagram 120 shows the slides when the ball is passed from "B" to "F." Number 1 drops to the foul line to prevent the pass from "F" to post, #5 takes "F," #4 takes the halfway position between the center of the foul line and the right corner and #3 plays toward the ball with his left foot on the foul circle line. The important move which we have added is being executed by #2 who is moving toward a position in front of the hoop similar to the wing-man move on our 3 out defense.

Diagram 121 shows the defensive positions when the ball is at "F."

Diagram 122 shows the slides when the ball is passed from "F" to "J" in the corner.

When "F" passes to "J," #5 pivots toward the ball and drives back toward the hoop; #4 slides to the corner and covers "J"; #1 slides out to the sideline at "F" for the cutoff play while #3 moves back to the foul line and protects the middle area and #2 moves to a position directly in front of the hoop thus completing the modified wing-man move. The defensive positions with the ball in the corner at "J" are illustrated in Diagram 123.

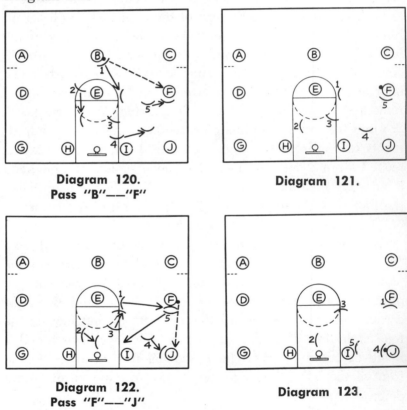

Diagram 120.
Pass "B"——"F"

Diagram 121.

Diagram 122.
Pass "F"——"J"

Diagram 123.

Keeping It Simple. The moves just explained are very simple and effective. They are exactly the same as our basic defense, in fact, we try to keep everything in our overall defense basically the same with just a few minor adjustments. We believe the less complicated we make things the easier it is for the players to master their defensive moves. The defense we have just explained made it a bit easier for the back line, for the simple reason that we keep #3 in the foul circle area. This takes care of the middle, and the back-line men do not have to make the slide to cover the middle.

If and when we instruct #3 to play the post man—man-for-man--no matter where he goes, he will sometimes leave the middle, taking #3 with him. This leaves the middle post area open for another man to flash into it. When this happens the back line must play its standard two back slides and go up and cover the post when the ball comes into a flashing post man as illustrated in the following diagrams.

Diagram 124 shows #3 covering "E" at the top of the foul circle, man-for-man. We will assume that "E" moves out and #3 still covers man-for-man as shown in Diagram 125.

When "E" moves out toward the vicinity of "D" and #3 continues to play "E" man-for-man, "H" moves up to the post position (or any other offensive man could move into the post position) and "B" passes to "H." The slides are as follows: #4 moves up and takes "H," #5 drops behind #4 and in front of the hoop, #2 drops back to the halfway point and #1 drops toward "H" for a possible double-team with #4 on "H." The positions with the ball at the post ("H") and "E" pulled out with #3 playing him man-for-man are shown in Diagram 126.

As you look at this setup, it appears that the right side of the court is wide open. This area can be covered by dropping #2 straight back toward the hoop and keeping #5 at the halfway point on the right as shown in Diagram 127. Remember, if "E" who is the good post man can be forced out of his key position, then you are forcing your opponents to use a less effective post man—perhaps one who is not as strong and ex-

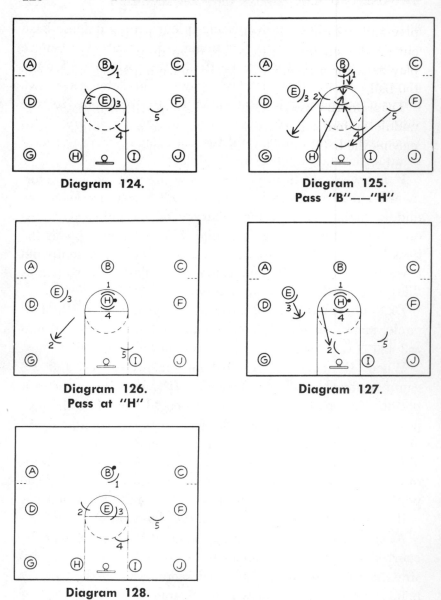

Diagram 124.

Diagram 125.
Pass "B"——"H"

Diagram 126.
Pass at "H"

Diagram 127.

Diagram 128.

perienced (we feel you can then double-team the original post man and not lose any defensive effectiveness). With the same play and #2 dropping straight back toward the hoop and #5 out on the sideline, #3 can afford to drop off from "E" and play zone for a moment and then move out on "E" if he gets the ball.

Diagram 128 has the 2-1-2 zone setup with #3 playing the middle or foul circle area. We will raise a few questions by moving the ball by the letters and you move the defense by the numbers.

SELF-TESTING QUIZ

PASS

1. "B"——"F"   1. 1, 5 (Example)
2. "B"——"F"——"J"
3. "B"——"F"——"J"——"I"
4. "B"——"F"——"J"——"E"
5. "B"——"F"——"J"——"F"

This is Quiz 3. Answers on page 210.

6

Combination or Change of Pace from Zone

A coach may find that it might be desirable to alter the sliding zone somewhat in order to meet some specific need. There were times when we modified our basic defenses slightly in order to cope with an outstanding shooter, playmaker or a peculiar type of offense. However, it should be noted that we usually got better results when we stayed close to our basic defensive plans than when we tried to incorporate variations in guarding style. Some of the combination defenses we used are as follows:

1. Four Man Zone–One Man Man-for-Man
2. Two Out Play Man-for-Man–Three Back Zone
3. Two Out Play Zone–Three Back Man-for-Man
4. Three Out Man for Man–Two Back Zone
5. Three Out Zone–Two Back Man-for-Man
6. Man-for-Man Pickup from within the Zone

FOUR MAN ZONE–ONE MAN MAN-FOR-MAN

This defense evolves from the basic 2 out 3 back zone with one front man playing man-for-man against a good shooter or key ball handler. The general purpose in having one man assigned to guard a particular offensive player is to create an element of confusion among the offense. The key player, one who is capable of controlling the offense by his passing and leadership abilities, should be harassed and guarded with such intensity that his teammates find it difficult to get the ball to him and vice versa.

It takes an agile and quick defensive man to play this position. In addition he must be skillful enough to play without committing fouls. One danger of this defense is that it may cause the offense to change its regular tactics and resort to another type of offense which may prove to be tougher.

We employed this defense with great success against the University of Pittsburgh's All-American Don Hennon. Our book on him was that he liked to shoot right-handed jump shots from anywhere and the hook shot only when he was going to his right. Our man playing him man-for-man held him to two field goals by near-arm guarding and keeping his hand in front of the ball when Hennon got ready to shoot. Seeing the hand there, he elected to pass instead of shoot. This enabled our defense to hold Don to his lowest field goal output.

Diagram 129 illustrates the basic 2 out 3 back defense with #1 playing man-for-man and the other four defensive men playing their regular defensive slides with one exception. The other front man, #2, will assume his position on the side of the court nearest the ball and play the position vacated by #1.

It is the job of #1 to play "A" man-for-man wherever he goes with or without the ball. If "A" passes to "E" and moves to the corner, #1 must go with "A" to the corner; #2 will

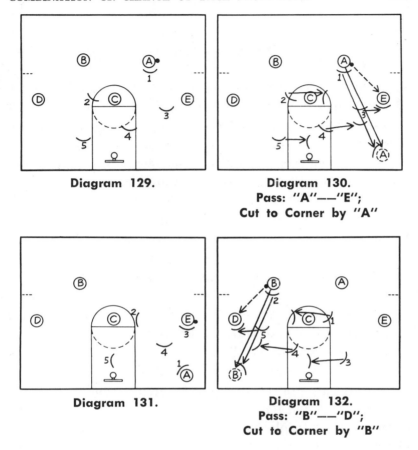

Diagram 129.

Diagram 130.
Pass: "A"——"E";
Cut to Corner by "A"

Diagram 131.

Diagram 132.
Pass: "B"——"D";
Cut to Corner by "B"

adjust slightly moving over to the right side of the foul circle and then execute his regular defensive slides. The three back-line men play their standard three back defense. Diagram 130 illustrates "A" going to the corner covered by #1 with the slides being executed by the other defensive men.

Diagram 131 shows the defensive alignment with the ball at "E" and "A" in the corner covered by #1. You will note that all moves are exactly the same as used in our regular 2 out 3 back sliding zone. The difference is that #2 moves over and plays the position left vacant by #1 who is playing man-for-man. In this maneuver we are taking advantage of the well-known defensive technique of "sloughing" away from the ball.

If "B" has the ball and we want #2 to play "B" man-for-man, the defensive procedures would be the same on the other side of the court. Defensive man #2 will follow "B" to the corner or wherever he might go, with or without the ball (see Diagram 132).

As seen in Diagram 132, player #1 moves to the left of the foul circle and plays the position vacated by #2. Players #3, #4, and #5 make their regular slides to the left side of the court. It may be more advantageous if you have a good man-for-man player in the position of #1 to designate him to cover "B"; then #2 must drop back and play the position for #1. In other words, #1 and #2 switch positions. This defensive maneuver combines some man-for-man with the sliding zone moves and also utilizes the "sloughing" technique. We have had excellent results with this and have held many top scoring threats to just one or two field goals.

TWO OUT PLAY MAN-FOR-MAN–THREE BACK ZONE

This is a combination in which the two front-line men play man-for-man and the three back men employ our three back zone slides. This type of defense can be quite effective if you know your opponents and their type of offensive formation. For example, if you know your opponent has two good shooting backcourt men and they do not employ a lot of maneuvers in order to operate in close to the hoop, you can well afford to play them man-for-man and keep your stronger rebounders back near the hoop. It is evident that when the two front men are pulled out to play man-for-man the post position at the foul line will be exposed. This is due to the eliminating of the staggered line effect. One man is up and one man is back. This void at the foul line may also pose a problem for your back-line

men. That is, there may be some confusion as to which man
should move forward to guard the pivot area. The best rule
to follow is: have the back-line man on the side the ball is on
move forward (see Diagram 133).

We employed this defense along with our standard 2-1-2 zone
with excellent success against Purdue and their fine All-American Terry Dischinger. The two front men were able to hold
Purdue's backcourt shooters in check. Our back line was able
to play straight zone, without shifting, while the back line
waited for Dischinger to roll toward the hoop. When he did
roll the back line was in excellent position to cover him. When
we switched to our basic 2-1-2 zone the man playing Dischinger concentrated on preventing the ball from getting into
him at the post position. The combining of these two defenses
limited Dischinger to three field goals, one of the lowest out-
puts of his career.

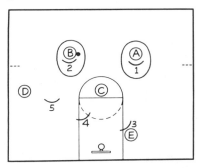

Diagram 133.

Diagram 133 shows #1 and #2 playing man-for-man against
"A" and "B" respectively while #3, #4 and #5 play a 3 back
zone with #5 in the "UP" position because in this case the
ball is at "B" on the left side of the court. If the ball should be
directly in the center of the court, the back-line men must
determine which man is "UP." This can be done very effectively after the offense has established its offensive pattern.
The rule to follow when the ball is in the center of the court
is to play where the offense is strongest and most likely to

play the ball. Notice how post man "C" is open from the front. This defense should only be employed when you are sure your opponents will not hurt you from the post. You should have information from your scouting reports.

TWO OUT PLAY ZONE–THREE BACK MAN-FOR-MAN

This formation is the reverse of the tactic just described. We get much better coverage on the post man with the two front men making their regular 2 out slides and the 3 back men playing man-for-man. Use of the back-line man-for-man coverage is particularly effective against a team lacking overall speed or cleverness in close to the hoop. The back-line men must be quick enough to gamble for the interception and to recover smartly when they do not get it.

We employed this defense against West Virginia when they had Rod Hundley. West Virginia would try to set up outside screens for him to shoot over. The 2 man zone out front defeated their screen attempts and as a result Hundley was denied his best shot. Hundley then chose to dribble, and spent more time dribbling than shooting. We felt this was a key factor in aiding us to an upset win over West Virginia. The Mountaineers' two big strong boys underneath were contained by our man-for-man coverage played by the 3 back men. Diagram 134 shows the defensive alignment of 2 out zone, and 3 back man-for-man.

In Diagram 134, #2, playing zone, covers "B" with the ball; #1 slides to the top of the foul line with a hand in front of "C," the post man; #4 is playing "C" man-for-man, giving us added defensive strength against the post man; #5 plays man-for-man on "D"; and #3 picks up "E" man-for-man. The back line can play straight man-for-man and not switch or they may switch, whichever is more successful. If switching tactics are preferred and "D" and "E" exchange positions, #3 can stay

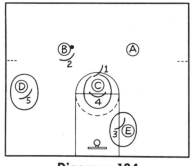

Diagram 134.

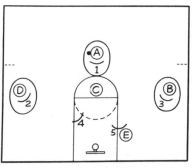

Diagram 135.

where he is and pick up "E" as "E" takes "D's" place. The same tactic may be used if "E" and "C" exchange places. Number 4 can pick up "E" in the post and #3 can pick up "C" along the lane line.

THREE OUT MAN-FOR-MAN–TWO BACK ZONE

We have had success employing combinations from our 3 out 2 back sliding zone as this is our active defense from which is launched full- and half-court presses. With man-for-man pressure out front we are attempting to force the offense into errant passes or poor shots. In order to use this defense successfully, it is imperative that you have two back-line men who can control the defensive backboard and get the rebounds. Otherwise we would not recommend using this defense. The 3 out man-for-man, 2 back zone defense can force an offensive team whose strategy is to control the tempo of the game out of their set pattern into a hurried style of play.

Practically every team we have played used a 1-3-1 attack against us at sometime during the game. We have had excellent defensing results with the 3 out man-for-man and the 2 back zone against the 1-3-1 offense by employing the movements seen in Diagram 135. With the ball at "A," #1, #2, and #3 play man-for-man. The two back-line men (#4 and #5) play their regular 2 back zone slides described in Chapter 4. This defense gives good coverage on the post man.

THREE OUT ZONE—TWO BACK MAN-FOR-MAN

In this defense the 3 out men play zone utilizing the 3 out slides with #1, the point man, dropping back to protect in front of the post position at the foul line. Meanwhile #4 and #5 play man-for-man. This defense is very effective against an offensive team which tries to exploit the outside by using one of the following offensive techniques:

1. A dribble-weave out front.
2. A 3 man figure 8 pattern out front.
3. Outside screens for a good shooter.

We had exceptional success with this defense against Syracuse University when they had Dave Bing. Syracuse worked awfully hard trying to set him up for the outside shot. Our employing the outside zone moves of the 3 out prevented them from screening us and getting Dave free for his shot. We did not stay exclusively with this defense against Bing. When he would go to the corner we had to shift into our 3 back zone. The reason for this shift was respect for Bing's great ability to drive along the baseline from the corners. Our theory was to get as many men as possible between Bing and the hoop congesting the area so much that there would be no room for him to drive. We were successful in four out of the six games Bing played against this defense.

Diagram 136 shows the 3 out zone and 2 back men playing man-for-man. Note that when the ball is passed from "A" to "D" #1 must drop back and protect the post position at the foul line. Number 3 can start for his position under the hoop (setting up the 3 back zone).

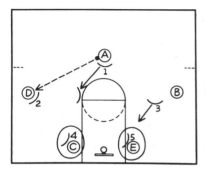

Diagram 136.
Pass: "A"——"D"

MAN-FOR-MAN PICKUP FROM THE ZONE

We have often shifted from our zone formation into a total man-for-man coverage. It is a simple procedure to shift from any of our basic zone formations and play man-for-man. The switch from zone to man-for-man is most effective when an opponent is operating from a "set" offense. It is not advisable to try this tactic against a team which employs a moving or revolving offense because of the tendency for the defensive players, as they follow the offensive players man-for-man, to be pulled out of the positions they play best. We stay in this man-for-man shift as long as it is effective or until the offense begins to move out of its set offense.

This type of defense was successful against a strong Naval Academy team. Their tactic offensively was to cut one man through the defense and have him go to the opposite side, setting up an overload formation. From this formation they would work the ball around in a very methodical pattern trying to get the ball to an open man, at a certain prescribed spot, before the zone defense player could make the slide. If they beat us at this maneuver, they would get the easy shot. Our strategy was to set up in a zone, but play the nearest offensive man, man-for-man. As long as they remained in their set offense it was a simple matter for our defense to cover them with a man-for-man.

SUMMARY

The defenses we have just discussed are all necessary to the overall team defense. We keep the changes as closely related to our basic defense as possible. We feel little changes of formation, changes of pace, mixing and matching man-for-man, along with combining man-for-man and zone give us a more complete defensive system which is flexible enough to cope with the many variations of offense.

Part III

Zone Presses—The Attacking Defenses

7

Sliding Zone Full-Court Press:
Three Out—Two Back

The full-court press is the most active defense available and it is especially successful when applied after the opponents have scored a field goal or a foul goal. The time that it takes for the ball to go through the hoop and be passed in bounds allows the defense to get into the "pressing defense" position.

The *main purpose* of any press is to get the ball and a quick basket as the result of an interception or steal. In addition we have found that it can be very helpful in speeding up our own team, particularly on a night when the team may appear to be a bit sluggish or tense. It is our "must" defense when we are trailing in the latter part of a game, but we have used it many times at the start of a game to surprise our opponents in an attempt to distract them from their game plans. Often this has given us an early lead and permitted us to control the tempo of the game. Finally, we have used it as a means of getting the ball when our opponents were using freezing or stalling tactics.

When we first started using a pressing defense, we attempted to match individual abilities on a man-for-man basis. If the offensive team got the ball over mid-court, we would go into one of our basic zones, either two out–three back or three out–two back. Fortunately we had ample time to set up because the offense, intent on getting the ball over the mid-court line, would stop their advance, reorganize, and then try to run through some predetermined patterns. Today, however, the offense moves the ball down court, tries to create outnumbered situations of 2-on-1 or 3-on-2 and get the shot off before the defense can get back and reorganize into a team defense. We feel that our press has been altered to counteract these moves by the offense although it is still relatively simple in design. Basically we use a 3 out–2 back sliding zone and try to cover the entire court, adding only a few assignments which we feel are necessary for defending the entire court. Assuming that our best defensive "pressers" are being used and that we know which offensive personnel are poor ball handlers, dribblers, and foul shooters, our objectives are to cover specific areas and to minimize the overload (2-on-1 or 3-on-2) situations.

COURT AREAS TO BE COVERED

Diagram 137 shows the court areas to be covered. The frontline numbers 1, 2 and 3 cover the areas shown. Number 1 is responsible for the left area from the left foul lane line extended to mid-court to the left sideline as shown. Number 3 is responsible for the right area from the right foul lane line extended to mid-court to the right sideline. Number 2 is responsible for the foul lane extended to mid-court. Numbers 5 and 4 are responsible for covering the near court, to anticipate the long pass, or in general, to try to prevent any pass from traveling the entire length of the court. You will notice in this

BALL ●

Diagram 137.

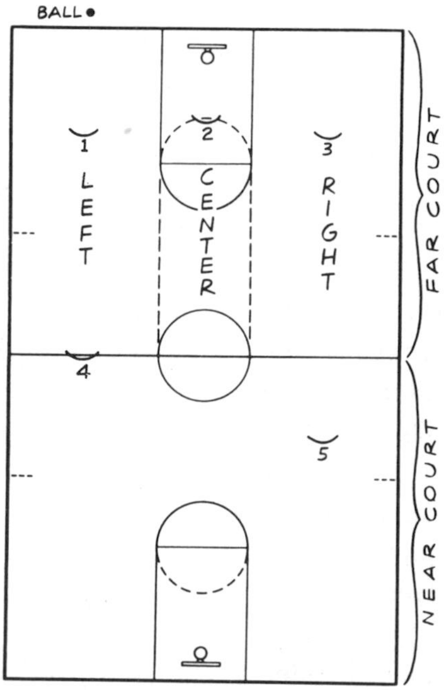

diagram that #4 is closer to the ball than #5. If the ball (or attack) was located on the right side of the court the positioning of #4 and #5 would be reversed.

We use our fastest and most agile men in the front line and the taller or heavier men in the near court area. There are times when we have reversed this procedure, playing our big men up in the far court. The reasons for this maneuver will be explained later. Now that we have designated the areas to be covered, we depend greatly on the type of defensive basketball which we discussed in the earlier chapters. The skills and aggressiveness of the players must be utilized while being alert to the fact that no one passes, catches, or dribbles the ball perfectly every time. The big factor which we feel is working for us when the opponents are preparing to put the ball in play is that on the court area the defense has the offense outnumbered. This is the only time that this situation ocurs. However, the area to cover has not lessened any and certain adjustments need to be made to capitalize on the five defensive against four offensive players setup.

RULES FOR PRESSING

We usually do not go up to the baseline and put pressure on the man who is out-of-bounds with the ball. We instruct our front men in the far court to drop back as long as there is no offensive man in front of them in their area of responsibility. They should drop back with their arms out so they can feel if a man comes in from behind them. They may drop back as far as the mid-court line, but should stay ready to move up toward the ball as soon as an offensive man comes into their area. When an offensive player does enter an area of responsibility the defensive man must pick him up immediately and smother him so the pass cannot get to him. If all three front men execute this maneuver correctly, it will force the man with the ball to throw the long pass over the front men and give our back-line men (#4 and #5) a chance to intercept or deflect the pass.

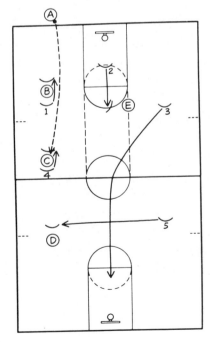

Diagram 138.

FORCING LONG PASS IN

Diagram 138 shows the back-line man #5 coming over to protect toward the goal and the sideline and the far front man #3 coming down the middle to protect the key area. Also in diagram 138 the pass from "A" to "C" is illustrated with #1 coming up to smother "B," #2 dropping back to cover "E," and #4 moving up to intercept the pass from "A" to "C." Number 5 will move to the left sideline to protect behind offensive player "C." Defensive player #3 moves through the center circle to the dotted line in front of the hoop. If the ball were played in from the other side of the court, #3 would cover on the right the same as #1 did on the left and #1 would make the move down through the center of the court to the dotted line. Number 2 will make the same moves as he did before, but #5 will come up to try for the interception and #4 will come over to protect at the right sideline.

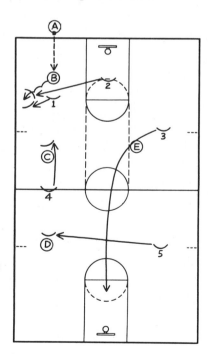

Diagram 139.
Pass: "A"——"B";
Dribble to Sideline

DOUBLE-TEAM ON SIDELINE

If the ball comes in from "A" to an offensive man in front of defensive man #1, 2, or 3, we encourage the man who receives the first pass to dribble; and then we force him to the sideline or to the middle. We will try to double-team him on the sideline or at the lane line in the center of the "far court." Diagram 139 illustrates the double-team on the sideline.

As "B" receives the pass and starts his dribble toward the sideline #1 cuts him off at the sideline and guards him aggressively. Number 2 comes over to help double-team. These two defensive men must play the offensive man "tough and tall" to force him to throw an errant pass, or a high pass which will be of help to the other defensive men in their effort to intercept. When the double-team occurs, #3 moves in front of "E" looking for the interception before he starts his move toward the hoop. Numbers 4 and 5 make the same moves as they did in Diagram 138.

DOUBLE-TEAM AT LANE

Diagram 140 shows the play if "B" dribbles to the lane; #1 stays with "B" and #2 comes up to doube-team as soon as "B" reaches the left lane line. The other defensive men, numbers 3, 4, and 5, make the same moves as they did in Diagram 139 always remaining alert and ready to make the interception.

TRAPPING

The most effective play for the defense is trapping on the sideline as shown in Diagram 139. As "A" moves onto the court from the end line to receive a return pass from "B" he can only move to his left toward the foul lane area and the

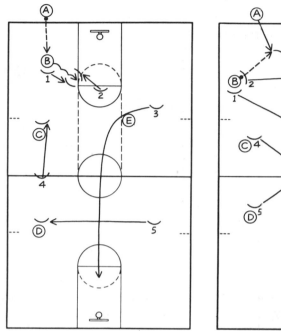

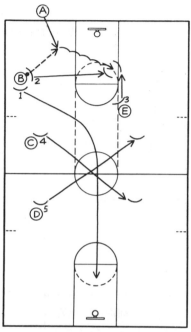

Diagram 140.
Pass: "A"——"B";
Dribble to Foul Lane

Diagram 141.
Pass: "B"——"A"; Double-Team
on "A" at Lane Line

right far court. When this happens, #2 goes with the pass and stays with "A." Number 3, who is in front of "E" must come up and help #2 double-team "A" at the right lane line. Number 5 must move up and over to the right side of the court. Number 4 moves over and back to protect behind #5. Number 1 will then make the move through the middle and to the dotted line as shown in Diagram 141.

Two Ways. When "B" is double-teamed on the lane line as shown in Diagram 140, the defense will have a tough job covering the play if the ball is passed from "B" to "A" as he enters the court. Offensive player "A" can go two ways, either right or left. Diagram 142 shows "A" receiving the pass from "B" and going to his right. As the return pass is made from "B" to "A" and "A" dribbles toward his right to the sideline,

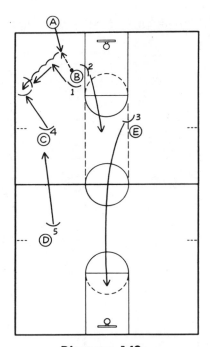

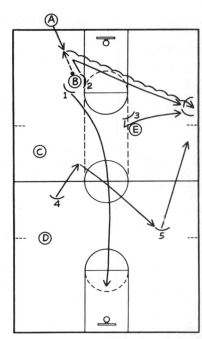

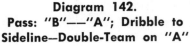

Diagram 142.
Pass: "B"——"A"; Dribble to
Sideline—Double-Team on "A"

Diagram 143.
Pass: "B"——"A"; Dribble to
Opposite Sideline Double-Team on "A"

#1 goes with the pass and picks up the dribbler "A" and forces him toward the sideline where #4 will come up to double-team. Number 2 must start back toward mid-court and #3 must take his usual path through the center heading for the defensive hoop and the dotted line. Number 5 will move up toward the double-team looking for an interception.

If "A" dribbles to his left after receiving the pass from "B" the moves are reversed. (See diagram 143.) Number 2 will go with the pass and pick up the dribbler forcing him to the right sideline. Number 3 will move over to the sideline and help #2 double-team "A" at the sideline. Number 1 starts his move through the middle and toward the dotted line in front of the defensive hoop, while #5 comes up to meet the attack as shown. Number 4 first moves up near "C" until he can read the play—"A" dribbling toward the right sideline pulling #5 up.

Number 4 then moves back through center court to the position vacated by #5.

LOOPING

Looping is a maneuver we employ when the ball gets out of the trap being set by the double-team maneuver and is caught up court by "C." This maneuver is shown in Diagram 144. As the ball is passed from "B" to "C," #4 covers "C" and gets between "C" and the basket. Number 1 will go directly with the pass and double-team "C" from the rear. Number 2 will then "loop" back toward the hoop passing by the trap or double-team. Number 3 will drive back toward the defensive hoop for a position at the dotted line and #5 will come over to protect near the left sideline.

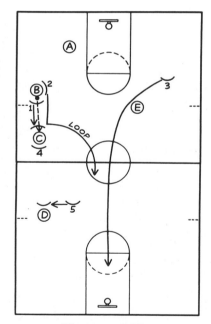

Diagram 144.
Pass: "B"——"C";
with #2 Looping

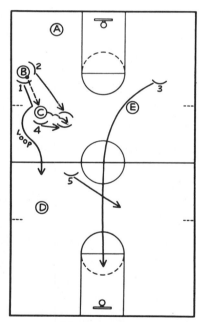

Diagram 145.
Pass: "B"——"C";
with #1 Looping

Note that the looping and the move by #3 toward the play and down the middle of the court to the dotted line in front of the hoop provides us with a continual defensive flow ahead of the ball. We maintain pressure on the ball and try to force a high pass or a bounce pass hoping to intercept it. The men looping or flowing down court should always keep alert looking for the interception. Our main objective is to get the ball. We do not care where we get it, just so we do get it! We have found that if the man playing the right front position (#3) paces himself according to the flow of the ball, he will make more interceptions between the foul line and the dotted line. This is because the offense will try to establish the outnumbered situation of 2-on-1 or 3-on-2 about where #3 cuts through at the dotted line of the foul circle. Number 1 will be the man making this move if the offense takes the ball down the other side of the court.

Number 4 will pick up "C" if "B," in the trap, passes to "C." Number 2 will come up to double-team "C" with #4 if "C" dribbles to the center of the court. Number 1 will then execute the loop to the outside of the court. This allows #5 to shift to mid-court; #3 still makes his moves to the dotted line. Diagram 145 illustrates #1 looping to the outside.

PRESSING DEFENSE AGAINST THE CROSS-COURT ATTACK

Many teams use the cross-court pass as a tactic in trying to break the zone press. We welcome and encourage any long pass because of the time it gives our defensive men to readjust. The longer the pass the greater the chances are for a possible interception. Diagram 146 shows the slides which are executed to counter a cross-court attack. "A" passes to "B" on the left side who in turn passes cross court to "E" before the trap is closed by #1 and #2. Number 3, who is starting his move through the middle, must make a quick analysis. If he anticipates that the pass is going to be returned to his side of the court he should try for the interception. His other choice of action would be to force "E" to the right sideline. In this case,

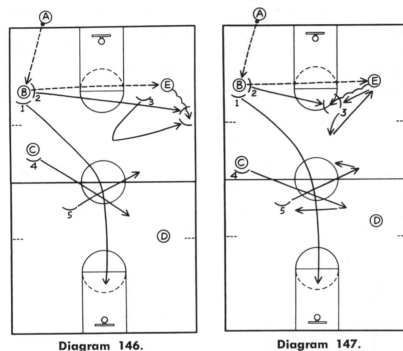

Diagram 146.	Diagram 147.
Pass: "A"——"B"——"E";	Forcing "E" to Middle;
Trap on Right Sideline	Trap by 2 and 3 at Top of Foul Circle

#2 who was trying to trap with #1 at "B" must come over to the right side and help #3 double-team "E" on the sideline. Number 5 will advance to the mid-court line ready to pick up anyone in front of him. Number 4 comes to the near court and plays the back position. Number 1 slides through the middle of the court on his way to the near foul line.

When the ball is at "E" and #3 can force "E" to come into the middle area, #2 can trap "E" with #3, at the foul circle. This makes the slide for #2 much shorter. The other men, numbers 1, 4, and 5, will adjust their slides accordingly (see Diagram 147).

It is important to note that when "E" dribbles to the middle of the court, #1 must use his judgment whether to continue to the near foul line or to delay momentarily and look for a pass coming out of the trap into his area. Numbers 4 and 5 will help him make up his mind. The positions they take may tell him to go for the near foul line. If they are pulled up by a pass or dribble into their area of responsibility, #1 will have to come back toward his starting position.

POINT MAN PRESSURE

We will throw in a variation of the full-court pressing defense when a team starts to beat the defense or if they call time out to set up an offense which they figure can penetrate. We will surprise them by guarding them right at the baseline, putting pressure on the ball with our point man or middle man

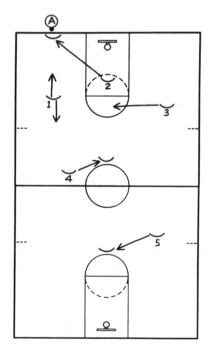

Diagram 148.

#2. We will utilize a tall, agile, long armed boy playing this spot so it will be more difficult for "A" to pass in bounds or to throw over #2. (See Diagram 148).

An open spot in the middle is created when #2 moves from his middle position and goes up to check "A." Therefore, #3 must come over and compensate for #2's absence. Number 1 must use his judgment and play up or back as the play dictates. Number 4 moves over to center court and #5 drops back near the top of the foul circle. This places #4 and #5 in the big three-against-two situation with #3 or #1 coming back to help out wherever needed.

SIMPLIFIED METHOD FOR TEACHING PRESS

We have found that one of the simplest ways to teach these pressing formations is to begin at the foul shooting line-up. A player from the team that is to use the full-court zone press will shoot the foul. After the foul has been made, the scoring team now on defense moves quickly into its zone press formation. Pressing after a foul shot gives the players sufficient time to think about their assignments and it has proved to be an organized way of practicing the press. After the team has become somewhat proficient in the use of the zone press, they may practice their pressing tactics in other game-like or scrimmage situations.

SUMMARY

Remember:

1. Begin teaching the full-court press from a foul shooting formation since it enables the players to quickly assume their defensive positions. After the players become more adept at assuming their positions, practice the pressing defense in regular scrimmage.

2. Encourage the defense to pressure the offense into dribbling to the sideline or to the lane line where double-teaming can take place.

3. Encourage all players to anticipate the long pass and to be ready to intercept.

4. On any dribble interchange by two offensive men have the pressers clamp the man with the ball.

5. Finally, remember that the full-court zone press is used to upset or surprise the opposition and to offset any sluggishness which may affect your team.

8

Spot Zones:
Full-Court and Half-Court Press

We have found it necessary to devise some adaptations for our standard full- or half-court presses. A smart team will begin to solve the problems posed by standard presses within a short time. The attack which confronts the full- and half-court defenses with the most trouble seems to be where the ball is passed into the center of the court and cuts are made along each sideline. When a team is successful with this maneuver we try to basically alter our preparatory starting positions in order to force the offense out of the middle. We then slide into our regular defense.

ONE-THREE-ONE SETUP

For example: we may set up in a full-court 1-3-1 formation matching the offensive setup being employed by the offense, in this case a 1-3-1. This defense is especially tough in the middle. While the ball is out-of-bounds, we place #1 (our point man) in front of the offensive man playing the middle while #5 plays directly in back of the middle man. So we are playing two men on one, before he gets the ball, and in this fashion force the first pass toward the sideline as shown in Diagram 149.

SWITCHING TO THREE OUT–TWO BACK

In Diagram 150 numbers 1 and 5 are playing "B" very tightly so that it is practically impossible for "A" to pass to "B." Numbers 2 and 3 take the inside positions and force "C" and "D" toward the sidelines. In this case "A" passes to "C" on the sideline. We now switch our defense from the 1-3-1 match-up to our regular 3 out 2 back full-court press, as explained in Chapter 7.

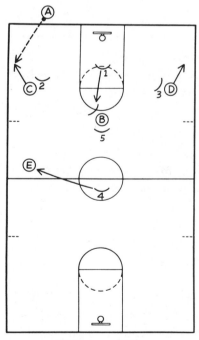

Diagram 149.

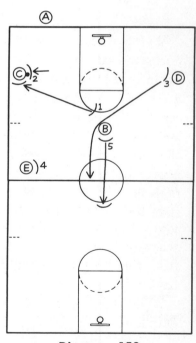

Diagram 150.

Double-Teaming. When "C" gets the ball, #1 must come over to help #2 double-team; #3 comes over toward the middle in front of "B" ready to make his move down court, anticipating any pass which might come from the trap. Number 4 has moved to "E" and #5 reads the play and can move back to his regular defensive position as soon as the regular front-line defense is formed in front of him, as shown in Diagram 150.

TWO-ONE-TWO MATCH-UP

Diagram 150 illustrates our regular full-court zone press as described in Chapter 7. We also use a 2-1-2 full-court match-up when the pivot man "B" is a roamer who moves from the middle to the sideline away from the ball. Notice that as #3 moves up to play "D" there is a lot of open area directly behind #3 in the far court area away from the ball. A strong, accurate baseball pass by "A" to "B" on the move may beat this press unless we match up as the ball is taken out-of-bounds and play a 2-1-2 forcing "B" to move toward the open spot; number 5 must be ready to come up and intercept the pass. It is also possible to double-team "B" at the sideline with #3 as shown in Diagram 151. Number 1 starts back toward the ball looking for any pass out of the trap or a pass back to "A" stepping in bounds. Number 4 moves over to protect behind #5 while #2 starts his move down the middle and toward the defensive hoop. The defensive moves necessary to cover the cross-court pass from "C" to "D" are the same as explained in Diagrams 146 and 147. Observing Diagram 150 you will notice that when the ball is at "C" the defense has made its initial move from the 1-3-1 formation and is now in our regular 3 out 2 back full-court press.

Double-Teaming on Sideline. Diagram 151 shows the double-teaming of "B" on the sideline by #3 and #5, a result

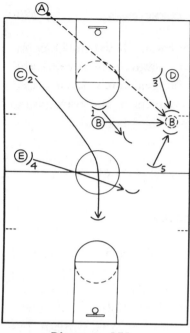

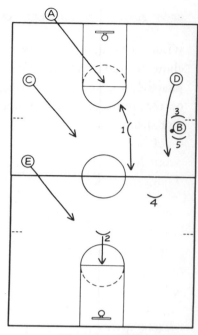

Diagram 151.

Diagram 152.
Ball at "B" in the Trap

of the 2-1-2 match-up. From here we mix into our regular full-court press as explained in Chapter 7. The play is exactly the same on the left side of the court, with #2 and #4 executing the trap.

When considering Diagram 152, assume that the offensive flow is moving toward the near court. The offense must get the ball over the mid-court line within ten seconds or they will lose possession of the ball. With this in mind note that #3 and #5 have put a trap on "B." In Diagram 152, #1 now becomes the key man. He must maintain a position between "B" and "C" (as "C" moves toward the near court) which will discourage "B" from passing to "C." He must force "B" to pass back to "A" and then be ready to pick up "A" and force him toward #3 for a possible trap with #3 at the front line. Number 3 must be ready to come back toward the mid-court line while #4 must move over to the left and #5 drop back as shown in Diagram 153. If this defensive maneuver is executed properly and causes a lot of action, a turnover or a violation of the ten-second rule by the offense often occurs. Diagram 152 shows the ball at "B" in the trap.

DEFENSE AGAINST POST MAN ATTACK

Many teams will also try to attack the half-court press by passing to a post man in the middle. Since the middle man is now relatively close to the basket, a subsequent handoff or pass to a teammate may set up a good shot. In other words, the defense has less time to react and adjust than when playing the full-court press. We often set up in a 1-3-1 or 2-1-2 defense and play tight in the middle, especially on the pivot man, when it is obvious that our opponents are getting the ball to the middle. We try to force the ball toward the sideline for traps

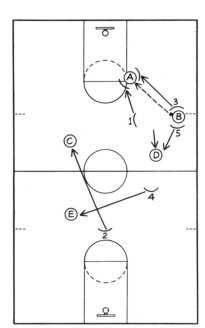

Diagram 153.
Pass: "B"——"A"

or a double-team on the ball. We then return to our regular 3 out 2 back half-court press. Usually we use these defenses when we are trailing in the latter part of the game. They are our desperation defenses. We expect our men to overplay, to take calculated risks, and to position themselves where their basketball instinct indicates a possible interception. This instinct is contingent upon the experience of the player, knowledge of his teammates' moves, and an ability to anticipate the moves of the opponents.

SUMMARY

We feel that when we are behind in a game almost anything is worth a try. But remember, the defensive principles discussed earlier must be kept foremost in mind no matter what team defense is tried.

9

Half-Court Sliding Zone Press:
Three Out—Two Back

Our half-court zone press from a three out–two back formation has proven to be a very interesting defense. It grew out
of a necessity to find a defense which would utilize most of
the team's abilities. We had completed a very successful
season the year before, but our most talented players had
graduated. They were players who were capable of playing
the full-court press and getting excellent results. After survey-
ing the material on hand, we decided we were only half as
good as we had been the past year and not fully capable of
playing a full-court press. We experimented with the half-
court press and found it to be very suitable for the abilities
of the remaining players.

LAUNCHING THE HALF-COURT ZONE PRESS

The Half-Court Zone Press begins much like a non-pressing

defense but quickly changes to a very active and aggressive defensive attack. We assume our normal defensive positions, explained for the three out–two back Sliding Zone, and wait until the offensive team bringing the ball up court approaches the ten-second line, or center court line. Just as they approach it with the ball, we move our front line out and hit them with the half-court press. This element of surprise at different intervals of the game often catches the offensive team napping and may upset them enough to turn over the ball to you a couple times before they can figure out what to do. We use this press to "speed up" our team which is also a purpose for using the full-court press. We use it as a probe to find out the opponent's weak ball handlers, and to attempt to control the pace of the game.

POSITIONS AND SLIDES OF HALF-COURT ZONE PRESS

The following explanations and diagrams show the positions and slides of the half-court zone press. Diagram 154 shows the attack from starting position hitting the offense at mid-court.

Defensive players #1 and #2 double-team "A" as he comes over the line at the left corner. We hope that it will be difficult for "A" to pass from the trap. Also we want the trap to be tight enough on the mid-court line to force a back-court violation or a jump ball situation. If the trap is tight enough on the side-line, we may force "A" into an out-of-bounds violation. You notice that this maneuver makes the court markings work in our favor. Number 3 who moved out toward the mid-court line on the initial attack, starts to retreat back with "B" as "B" comes over the line. If the pass does come in this direction, #3 must try to intercept it. Number 4 moves up toward the double-team trap in the area of "D" and tries to get in front of "D" to intercept any pass thrown to him. Number 5 will move up toward the post man "C" to intercept any pass in this direction.

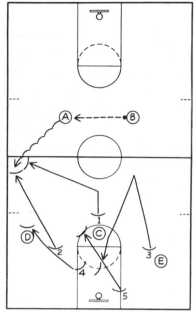

Diagram 154.

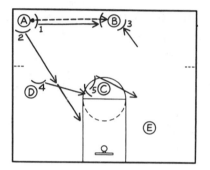

Diagram 155.
Pass: "A"——"B"

Defensing Pass from Side to Middle. Defensive slides to counter a pass from "A" to "B" are shown in Diagram 155. Number 3 moves forward looking for the interception. If there is no interception he checks "B" while #1 follows the pass and executes the double-team with #3 on "B." Number 5 moves in front of "E" on the right side of the court; he looks for a pass from "B" and a possible interception. Number 4 moves into the area vacated by #5 and guards the post man "C" with a hand in front being prepared to deflect the ball away or intercept any pass coming to "C." Number 5 must remain alert to protect under the hoop. Number 2 comes back toward the foul circle, toward "C," and will eventually come through the foul lane, toward the hoop should #4 be pulled toward the right sideline.

Defensive Coverage on Post Man. Assume that the pass is made from "A" in the trap to "C" at the post and #5 does not intercept. Number 5 now has to guard "C" at the post. The other moves are executed as follows (see Diagram 156): Number 5 guards "C" at the post by staying between "C" and the hoop while #1 slides back to the top of the foul circle and double-teams "C" with #5. Number 3 drops to the cutoff position halfway between the center of the foul line and the right corner. Number 4 moves quickly to a position in front of the hoop looking to defend against anyone who might enter the hoop area. Number 2 drops back toward the ball and then to the cutoff position on the left side of the court.

Defensing Pass Down Side and Overload. The pass from "A" out of the trap to "D" with "E" moving from the right side

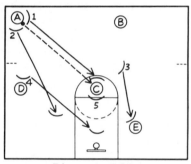

Diagram 156.
Pass: "A"——"C"

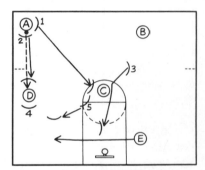

Diagram 157.
Pass: "A"——"D"

of the court to the left corner creates an overload situation. The importance of the move by the wing man #3 to the front of the hoop is obvious. Diagram 157 shows the overload situation and the crucial move by #3 to the hoop area. Number 4, if he cannot intercept the pass, must defend against "D" and try to force him to the sideline. Number 2 moves along with the pass and tries to double-team "D" with #4. Number 5 moves to the halfway point while #1 drops back toward the top of the circle to look for any pass to the area of "B" and also tries to cut off any pass at "C." Number 3 makes his move into the foul circle at "C" and then must use his own judgment whether to go (1) in front of "C," (2) between "C" and the ball which is at "D," (3) behind "C" or (4) to the right of "C" and down the lane for a position in front of the hoop. If #1 gets back in time and can cut off the pass, then #3 must go behind "C." If #1 is not back, #3 should try to intercept at "C" if at all possible.

The moves we have just explained and shown are practically the same as employed by the full-court press. The half-court press takes place in a more restricted area and the players do not have to loop and slide as far. It most certainly does not require as much energy, speed and skill to press half court as it does full court.

Bluffing the Passer and Covering Pivot. After a time our opponents become familiar with the moves of this defense and will get rid of the ball about a yard or two before they get to the mid-court line. Usually they will throw to the post man in the center who comes out at the top of the foul circle. This maneuver caused us some concern when it was first employed against this defense but we found a solution for breaking up this play. To prevent the pass from the back court into the high post we employ the moves shown in Diagram 158.

Number 1 goes out toward the man with the ball (in this case "A") and bluffs the double-team move. He then retreats quickly and goes for the top of the foul circle where he tries to intercept the pass to the post man. If he cannot intercept, he may be able to deflect the ball toward #2 or #3 as they come back. They should be alert for this play.

We work hard on this defense trying to keep the ball out of the middle or post position. Once the ball gets into the post it can be passed to either side of the court. This makes our defensive job twice as difficult. It we can force the ball to the sidelines, keep it at mid-court, in the corners or at baseline, we can usually double-team or force a lob pass, bounce pass or jump ball. From these spots we know the ball can only go in

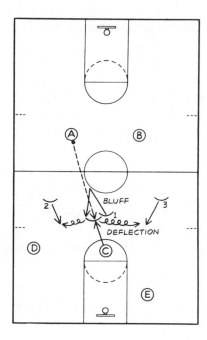

Diagram 158.

one direction. This gives our other defensive men a chance to position themselves where they may have a better chance to intercept the ball.

BENEFITS FROM THE HALF-COURT PRESS

Remember if the press does not get the ball, but is successful in "speeding up" our own team, discovering the opponent's weak ball handlers or changing the opponent's predetermined pace, then it has served some worthwhile purpose. Basically these are our 3 out 2 back Sliding Zone moves extended somewhat over the basic moves and cut down one-half from our full-court zone press. The back line must remember to play the big two-against-three and to be alert for a gamble on an interception. This is really a gambling defense; as long as it is getting the desired results, use it until your opponents appear to have it solved. Once they get a few easy baskets you will have to change to another formation. We have never been able to employ this defense for an entire game. It has been more useful in the situations we have explained and is very good for breaking up the stall or freeze.

IN SUMMARY: THE PRACTICE PROCEDURE

When we practice this defense we give the ball to the offensive team at the top of their own foul circle and let them advance the ball toward the defense. We make them go to each corner several times so that the defense can become familiar with the corner traps. We deliberately have the offense go to the high post in order to practice and learn the trap at mid-court as shown in Diagram 155. After we execute several of each situation, we then let the offense vary their attack and try to outmaneuver the defense.

10

Break Up the Stall from Any Zone

LACK OF ACTION

We have been involved in several games in which our opponents tried to get us out of our zone formation by stalling or freezing the ball. This was true especially when we were ahead. However, we would refuse to deviate from our zone defense. This, of course, resulted in very dull basketball. The fans and players did not like this type of game and the unfavorable comments and publicity resulting from games of this type forced the rules makers to insert rules which prevented stalling. (Today the rules have been changed and a team must come out after a warning from the officials.) Even with the anti-stalling rules, teams have still played a deliberate game against us, forcing us to go after them and get the ball. We maintain that if our pressing defenses are executed properly they will get us the ball and cause enough action. However, there are times when we need a change of pace from our regular defense and we have found the "break up the stall

defense" to be the answer. We can execute this defense from
any of our regular half-court defenses.

BREAK UP STALL FROM TWO OUT–THREE BACK ZONE

Assume we are employing our 2 out 3 back regular sliding
zone and a team stalls or freezes the ball on us. On a given
signal, one that the entire team understands, we move from
our regular 2 out 3 back into our Break Up The Stall Defense.

Diagram 159 shows the 2 out 3 back. We try to get the
offensive man "B" to pass to the side man "F" as shown. As
the pass is made, #1 goes right along with the pass and
double-teams "F" along with #3. Number 4 takes the halfway position and #5 protects in front of the hoop. Number 2
now has the key play to execute; he must get between "E"
and "F" and try to intercept any pass coming near "E" or back
out to "B." He can get there by going around "E" at the top
of the foul circle or coming around him at the foul line. Both
paths are shown. Our suggestion is to allow #2 to use his
preferred move. The play hinges on the work done by #1
and #3 who are double-teaming. They should attack "F" with
some force, trying to tie him up for the jump ball or making
it so difficult for "F" that he throws the lob pass or bounce
pass giving the other men in the defense a chance to intercept. Diagram 160 illustrates the defensive alignment when
the ball is at "F" and the double-team is on him.

Double-Team in Right Corner. Normally the pass will go to
"J" in the corner or back out to "B." If it goes to "J" in the
corner, #4 will take "J" and #3 will move along with the pass
to execute the double-team on "J" in the corner. Number 5
holds his position, #1 moves in front of "F" to cut off a return
pass and #2 takes a position with his left hand between "E"
and "J" in order to guard against a screen as he moves out from
"E" to "B." These moves are shown in Diagram 161.

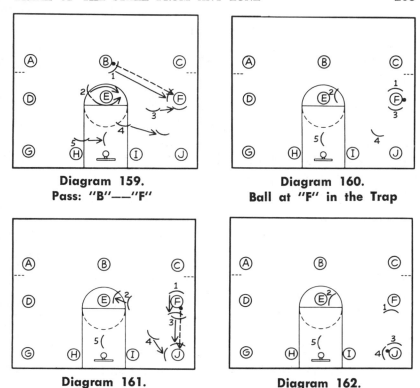

Diagram 159.
Pass: "B"——"F"

Diagram 160.
Ball at "F" in the Trap

Diagram 161.
Pass: "F"——"J"

Diagram 162.

Diagram 162 shows defensive positions when the ball is at "J" and the double-team is executed by #3 and #4.

Double-Team at Middle. In Diagram 163, "F" has the ball in the trap and he passes back out to "B." Number 2 must take "B" and #1 must move back with the pass to double-team "B" with #2. Number 3 moves to his left at the "UP" position of the foul line extended; #4 moves up to the foul line and #5 moves up to the left side at the foul line extended. The back-line men are actually overplaying and gambling on an interception. If #1 and #2 execute their double-team with vigorous skill, the interception will become a greater possibility. Diagram 163 shows the defensive moves when "F" is in the trap and passes back out to "B."

Movement to Far Side. If the ball is passed to the far side
from "B" to "D" before #2 and #1 can set the trap as shown
in Diagram 163, the defense must move as shown in Diagram
164. Number 5 starts to move up and to the left when the pass
is made to "B." When "B" passes to "D," #5 must move to
take "D" and, if possible, intercept the pass. Otherwise he
must set the trap with #2 who has gone up to cover "B." As
"B" passes to "D," #2 must change his direction and go with
the ball and set the trap on "D" with #5. Number 4 moves up
toward "E" and then to the left taking the halfway position.
Number 3 moves to the left to a position in front of the hoop
and favors "E." Number 1 moves out and then drops back to
a position at the top of the foul circle. Here he must play
halfway and gamble for the interception of a pass to "E" or
"B."

The positions with the ball at "D" are shown in Diagram
165.

Trap in Left Corner. If the ball is passed from "D" to "G"
the following slides must be made (see Diagram 166): Number
5 moves with the pass and sets the trap on "G" with #4 who
moved to the corner. Number 2 moves between "D" and the
ball to the cutoff position. Number 1 takes a position in front
of "E" and remains ready to roll back to "B" or over to the
right side of the court to cover "C" or "F." This long move is
very difficult and #1 must be careful not to get screened by
"E." If #1 can slide through and #4 and #5 trap correctly
forcing the high pass to the far side of the court, then #1 will
have a good chance for the interception or deflection. Number
3 moves to his left and takes a position to the left of the lane.
The positions with the ball at "G" are shown in Diagram 167.

Diagram 168 shows defensive positions with the ball at "B"
and #1 and #2 executing the double-team. If the double-team
is successful, the remaining defensive men should anticipate
high passes or desperation passes.

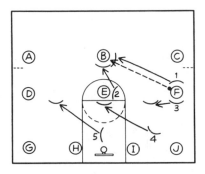

Diagram 163.
Pass: "F"——"B"

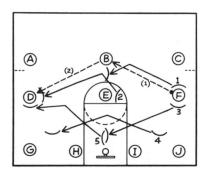

Diagram 164.

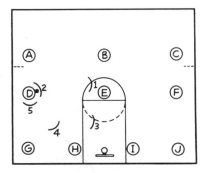

Diagram 165.
Positions when Ball Is at "D"
with #2 and #5 Trapping

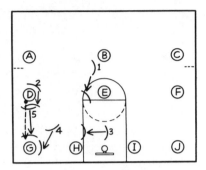

Diagram 166.
Pass: "D"——"G"

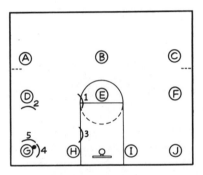

Diagram 167.
Positions when Ball Is at "G"

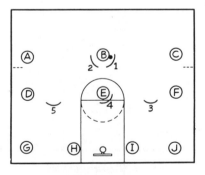

Diagram 168.
Ball at "B" in the Trap.

Trap on Left Sideline. In Diagram 169, "B" is covered by #1 and passes to "D" on the left sideline. Number 2 must "cheat" a little on his starting position because it is more effective to have #2 cover "D" than #1, should the pass be completed to "D." Number 1 must move along with the pass and close the trap or double-team with #2 at "D." Number 5 plays more toward the corner, #4 plays a step beyond the foul lane and #3 can use his own judgment according to where the other offensive men are playing. Number 3 should be able to sense where the pass may be thrown and then gamble for the interception. Diagram 169 shows these moves.

We have explained the moves with #1 and #2 trapping. Number 5 can also trap with #1 at "D." Number 2 can then stay in and protect the pivot area. Number 4 will have to come to the left and take the halfway position and #3 will have to take a position in front of the hoop. Both are effective methods. Which one to use is determined by the offensive formation being employed. If the offensive attack has a man in the corner at "G," perhaps it would be more advantageous to have #2 trap and #5 stay back ready to cover the corner.

Diagram 170 shows the defensive positions when the ball is at "D" in a trap closed by the double-teaming maneuver of #1 and #2.

Diagram 171 shows the moves when the ball is at "B"; "B" is covered by #1 and passes to "E" in the post. Number 4 comes up and takes "E" forcing him to turn away from the hoop; #1 goes with the pass and should get to "E" as "E" turns away from the hoop and into #1 who tries to steal the ball. Number 1 must be careful not to foul "E." We have found if #1 reaches in high and strikes or grabs down at the ball, he will have less success at stealing the ball, and will most often be called for fouling. However, we have discovered it to be more successful if he reaches in below the ball and inserts his arm between the offensive man's arms and reaches up toward the offensive

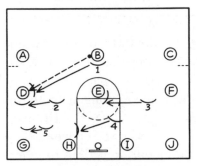

Diagram 169.
Pass: "B"——"D"

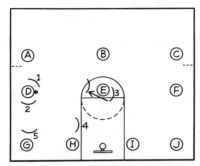

Diagram 170.
Ball at "D" in the Trap

man's chin and pulls outward. He will be more successful at dislodging the ball from the grasp of the offensive man. Also, this type of movement looks less like a foul and the tendency of the referees is to permit this type of action as opposed to the striking in and down movement.

Trap at Post. Diagram 172 shows the positions of the defense when the ball is at "E." Number 5 moves to a position in front of the hoop, #2 drops off toward the left corner, and #3 drops back toward the right corner. This is the same coverage we have in our 3 out 2 back defense when the ball is in the post position at "E" on the foul line.

Applying "Traps" and "Jabs." We have just explained the

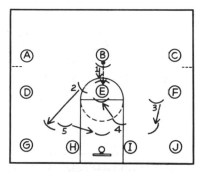

Diagram 171.
Pass: "B"——"E"

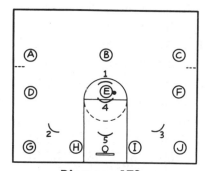

Diagram 172.
Ball at "E" in the Trap

basic moves of our "break up the stall defense." All of the logical passing plays have been covered. The only adjustment the defense would have to make is when the play originates from the center, off the sidelines, or from the corners. The slides are the same even if the offense works in closer to the hoop. The defense must remember to adjust to the position of the ball. When stalling, the offensive team has a tendency to stay out near the mid-court line. The "break up the stall" defense must move out after them with the back-line men ready to protect against the easy lay-in shot. The maneuvers explained must be a series of quick sharp attacks, like the "jab" in boxing—hit them quickly and then back to your regular defense. After reorganizing, allow a pass or two, then strike again. Remember, when on defense, it is better to have the offense pass the ball than shoot it. These "traps" and "jabs" can be executed from any of our basic defenses. Though we have used the 2 out 3 back for our explanation, the same rules apply for the 3 out 2 back and the 2-1-2 zones.

DEFENSING SPREAD OUT OFFENSE

It should be made clear at this point that the use of this type of defense for breaking up the stall cannot be sustained for too long a time, perhaps three or four times after the ball is brought over the middle line. We use this along with our regular half-court press as a quick maneuver or change of pace. If it gets us the ball two or three times we feel it has accomplished its purpose. We have found by using the combination of these two defenses that we will force the offense into a spread out offense, usually a 2-1-2. This spread makes breaking up the stall impossible because of the long slides. When the offense spreads out we play our regular half-court press and have the defensive men away from the ball play their regular defense as explained in Chapter 9. Remember that when two defensive men are on one offensive man there will be an offensive man free somewhere. It is the object of the trapped offensive man to get the ball to the free man. The free man's job is to get into an area where he can receive a pass. The defense must be aware of this four-against-three—that one offensive man is free and looking for the open area. The defense should protect the most easily accessible areas making it difficult for the passer to locate the open area and player. The defense should use basketball sense, splitting the difference between offensive men by positioning themselves in the accessible areas and be ready to gamble for the interception.

IN SUMMARY: GOING WITH THE PASS

The important difference and rule to remember when executing this defense is: The defensive man who is covering an offensive man who gets off a pass must go with the pass and put the double-team or trap on the receiver. This maneuver gets excellent results because the receiver does not expect to see a defensive man coming along with the pass. The sight of a defensive man coming along with the ball is one which both surprises and perplexes the offensive man because he will be looking for a possible chance to return the pass. You will be surprised to find the receiver attempting to pass right back to the man who passed to him and tossing the ball into the hands of the defensive man.

Part **IV**

**Auxiliary Techniques
for Certain Zone Success**

11

Out-of-Bounds Coverage by Zone

ALERTING THE DEFENSE

The defensive team must be extremely alert when the offensive team has the ball out-of-bounds in the offensive half of the court. This is no time for the defense to relax or fall asleep. The sight of the ball going out-of-bounds should be the signal for the defensive team to assume its defensive position and get set immediately by facing the ball and protecting the area near the hoop. In addition the strategy of the defense is to force the offensive man passing the ball in bounds to throw a high, long pass to the outer perimeter of the defense, a pass which the defense may have a chance to intercept. If the offense does catch the ball on the outer perimeter, they will be beyond the good shooting area and will need to pass the ball at least once more before taking a shot. Many times we will not apply defensive pressure on the man taking the ball out-of-bounds, but instead will guard 5 against 4 pressuring the 4 offensive men who are in bounds. There is, however, one important time when we must put pressure on the man out-of-bounds and that

is when we are in the closing seconds of the half or game. We
will have the nearest defensive man play the man out-of-bounds
as closely as the rules permit. We will have this man go right up
to the boundary line and use excessive arm gestures and movements, trying to deflect the pass or force an errant one. This
is a strategy used by many coaches in an effort to protect a one-
or two-point lead or to prevent the opponent from scoring the
winning basket from an out-of-bounds play.

DEFENDING AGAINST HIGH PASS TO BIG MAN AT HOOP

A very effective offensive play from out-of-bounds with only
a few seconds remaining is to pass the ball near the rim and
have a big man jump up to guide or drop the ball into the hoop.
To defend against this we cluster close to the hoop. We try to
get two men in this area before the big offensive man can get
his position. At the same time we move a big defensive man
up tight on the man taking the ball out-of-bounds. This defensive man must keep pressure on the man out-of-bounds, playing
as close to him as possible, keeping the arms up, waving to
distract the offensive man's vision, and perhaps deflecting the
ball. Diagram 173 shows defensive back-line men #4 and #5

Diagram 173.
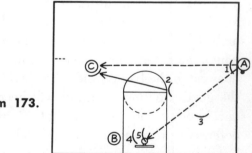

in position in front of the hoop in order to prevent the big man
"B" from controlling the high pass from "A" who is out-of-

bounds. Number 1 is pressuring the passer. Number 2 protects the general area in and around the foul circle. Number 3 protects the area from the right of the foul lane to the right sideline and corner. We are taking a gamble as this invites the long shot from out front or from the left. But these shots are preferred over the short lay-up or "dunk" shot by the big man. If the out-of-bounds man passes to the left side of the court to an open man we have our front man #2 go along with the pass and try to bother the shooter as much as possible.

We employ the same type of defense on all out-of-bounds plays, basically our 2 out 3 back zone. The following diagrams illustrate our defensive alignment when the ball is out-of-bounds, under the hoop, along the baseline, or on the sideline.

Diagram 174 shows our defensive setup when the ball is out-of-bounds under the hoop.

OUT-OF-BOUNDS UNDER THE HOOP

When "A" has the ball out-of-bounds under the hoop as shown in the Diagram 174, the defensive men #3, #4, and #5, our back line, form the pocket as shown. If "A" elects to pass to the left corner he will have a difficult pass. Should #5 keep his hands out and up, it is practically impossible for "A" to pass to the left corner because the backboard and rig which holds it will block his passing zone. This will force him to bounce pass into the corner giving our defense enough time to slide to the corner and cover any shot from there. Should "A" try to pass to the mid-court area beyond the perimeter of the defense, the defense will again have time to slide and cover the man who catches the ball. If "A" tries to throw to the right corner or right sideline, #3 should be able to force the high pass or bounce pass giving our defense time to slide and pick up the offensive man in the corner or outer perimeter. This defensive formation gives a very good coverage in the lane area and directly in front of the hoop.

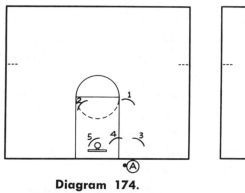

Diagram 174.
Ball Out under Hoop

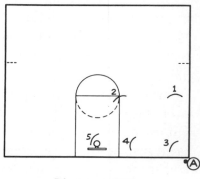

Diagram 175.
Ball Out in Corner

COVERAGE ON BASELINE NEAR THE CORNER

When the ball is out-of-bounds along the baseline near the corner or at the corner, our defensive alignment is as shown in Diagram 175.

Our back line keeps its strength between the ball and the hoop near the baseline. The front line positions are the same as in our regular defense when the ball is in the corner. We apply the same principles of our regular defense; hands up, force the high lob pass to the open areas around the outside of the defense.

COVERAGE ON SIDELINE

With the ball out-of-bounds on the sideline between the foul line extended and the corner (Diagram 176), our alignment remains about the same. Note the slight difference in player positioning when the ball is out-of-bounds between the foul line extended and the mid-court stripe (Diagram 177). All defensive men face the ball and remain in their basic 2 out 3 back zone. The basic difference shown in Diagram 177 is the position of #5, the far back-line man. With the ball at "A," an intended pass to an offensive player between #4 and #5 obviously must

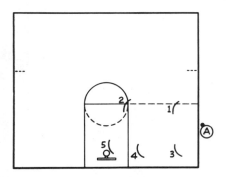

Diagram 176.
Ball Out on Sideline Between
Foul Line Extended and Corner

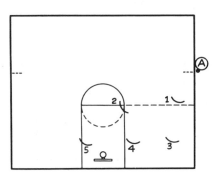

Diagram 177.
Ball Out on Sideline Between
Foul Line Extended and Mid-Court

be much longer than if "A" were nearer to the corner. There-fore #5 can afford to drop back to a position along the left lane line and look for a long pass between #4 and himself or for the long pass over the defense to the left corner.

PLAYING OFF THE BALL

When we are ahead, we play off the ball remaining passive until the ball comes in bounds. Then we try to take advantage of a lob, bounce, or errant pass or poor ball handling. If the game is tied, or if we are protecting a slight lead, we put pres-sure on the man out-of-bounds with the ball. If we are behind in the score and are pressing in order to get the ball, we employ the pressing strategy already explained in the chapters on the full- and half-court press using the five-against-four on the court theory.

DEFENSING SPECIAL PLAYS

There are many special offensive plays from out-of-bounds which may give a defensive team trouble. One such play evolves

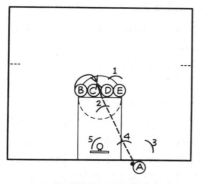

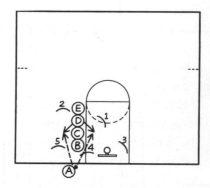

Diagram 178.   Diagram 179.

from a solid line formation along the foul line or a solid line formation along the foul lane line. Diagram 178 illustrates a solid line along the foul line with the ball out along the baseline. One of the offensive men in the solid line steps back toward the top of the foul circle and receives a pass from the out-of-bounds man while the other three members in the solid line close ranks and form a screen for him. As soon as the defense sees this formation setting up they must get into a fixed defense. The back line plays the same as always but the front line must play as shown in Diagram 178 with one man in front of the solid line and one man in back of it. Then, as the offensive man steps back, the defensive man will not be screened.

Number 1 is in position to prevent the shot by "B" and in most cases will prevent the pass from getting to "B." Number 2 should be able to prevent a pass from coming directly to any of the men who remain in the line, since they are quite close to one another. The presence of #2 usually forces all 3 men out of the foul line area. The back line turns with the ball as it is thrown over their heads. They will be in good defensive position for coverage of any of the men leaving the foul line area.

This same type of offensive play, when set up along the foul lane line is covered by the defense in somewhat the same fashion. Diagram 179 illustrates the solid line along the left foul lane line with the ball out-of-bounds under the hoop. The offensive strategy here is to form a solid line screen with one man moving to the hoop side of it for a lay-in shot, or behind it for a jump shot.

Number 4 must quickly secure his regular defensive position between the ball and the hoop with his right hand in front of "B." This will prevent the lay-up. Number 5 must not get caught inside toward the hoop or he will be screened and unable to stop the jumper from the right side. If #5 assumes the position shown in Diagram 179 he will be in position to stop the jump shot over the screen. Numbers 1 and 2 take positions on each side of the line, and wait until someone comes out of the line into their area. They then cover whichever player enters their area trying to prevent him from getting the ball. Out-of-bounds situations such as these occur about four or five times a game. There should be no excuse for easy baskets as a result of solid line screen plays.

12

Rebounding and Conversion
from Defense to Offense

Probably the most outstanding trademark of a good basketball player is his ability to rebound. Statistics point out that in most games 54 percent or more of the shots attempted from the field will be missed. This provides an opportunity for the good rebounding team to control the game.

REBOUNDING SKILLS

Rebounding requires a special skill which contributes much to ball possession. The technique used for successful rebounding depends on the height of the players, jumping ability, strength, timing, quickness of the hands and arms in securing and clearing the ball, and learning to protect the ball by assuming a body position which prevents the opponents from getting a hand on the ball. When size, jumping ability and skills are about equal, floor position will become the controlling factor.

The rebounder should be between his opponent and the basket, but not too far under the basket. The distance he should play out from the basket depends partly on the liveliness of the backboard and basket. Six feet out from the basket might be too far for a "dead" board and hoop but not far enough for a lively one. Before each game on a strange court, the player should consider board and hoop rebound distance. The coach should make the players aware of this factor.

Defensive Rebounding. The defensive rebounder has certain advantages over the offensive rebounder if he uses good defensive techniques. For example, by keeping between the offensive man and the hoop the defensive man will be closer to the basket and should have an unobstructed path when going after the rebound. The defensive man's rebounding form is slightly different from the form of the offensive rebounder.

Jack-Knife. One of the most successful body positions used when securing defensive rebounds is referred to as "jack-knifing." While in the air at the height of the spring the body is flexed at the waist with legs spread, knees bent, and arms and hands extended above the head to catch the ball. The "jack-knife" position is a common occurrence after ball recovery by a rebounder. It illustrates a sound technique; however, many big agile men find this position not only unnecessary to clear the ball, but too time-consuming for getting the offense started. Some defensive players tap the ball away from the board with one hand, then catch it in a more open area; others will tap the ball out to a teammate at a designated spot. With the offensive development of the tap-in shot, the two-handed "jack-knife" recovery has become more difficult to execute. The defensive man must have a decisive advantage of position in order to use the "jack-knife" technique. Photo 13 illustrates this technique.

Landing Technique. Landing in the preparatory position after jumping must be learned. If the player does not land in

Photo 13.   Jack-Knife Technique.

position for immediate initiation of the next appropriate move, he will be too slow to gain any advantage on the next play. Moreover, he is likely to suffer injury if he lands off balance. In jumping, the feet should not be tucked up to the body. It takes too long for the feet to make contact with the floor afterwards. The player is not only out of the next play longer, but less able to protect himself.

Defensive Rebounding Advantage. Another advantage for the defensive team is that more defensive men are available for rebounding since some of the offensive players must remain back to maintain balance. Team strategy for the defensive team may be to "crash" all five men toward the board when the offense shoots, hoping that the five men will overpower the usual three offensive rebounders. Such all-out "crashing" eliminates the opportunity for a fast break after a rebound. Diagram 180 shows the offensive rebounding position with two men back to guard against the fast break.

Offensive Rebounder (Slashing). The offensive rebounder facing these disadvantages has become more of a "slashing" straight body type of rebounder, keeping the ball up, tapping or guiding the ball into the hoop while he is still in the air; or while in the air getting control of the ball and hesitating or suspending himself in the air by giving a "kip-kick" of the feet with an extra flexion of the body. This tends to keep him up a while longer than the defensive men. He then can, from this suspended position, take a relatively unmolested shot at the hoop. Two outstanding players who have mastered this type of rebounding are Elgin Baylor and Jerry West of the Los Angeles Lakers. These two men are not the giant type rebounders but are effective rebounders because of the "kip-kick" technique and their ability to remain suspended in the air.

We have stressed floor position as one of the dominating factors in controlling the rebound. We feel that we can take advantage of the floor positions which our various zone formations afford us. We especially are able to control rebounding at the defensive end of the court. The following diagrams show our defensive rebounding positions from our basic zones.

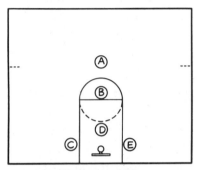

Diagram 180.
Offensive Floor Balance and Rebound Position

TWO OUT–THREE BACK REBOUND POSITIONS

Diagram 181 shows the desired defensive rebounding positions from the two out–three back zone.

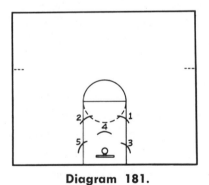

Diagram 181.

MEDIUM-LONG REBOUND

It is important to remember to form the rebound triangle near the hoop with back-line men numbers 3, 4, and 5. The front line, #1 and #2, must move in straddling the lane lines and at the dotted line of the foul circle. Numbers 1 and 2 must stay in their positions so they can control the medium-long rebound. They should not pull out of these positions and start to fast break until they are sure that one of their teammates has absolute control of the ball. One of the most important factors in winning any ball game is control of the medium-long rebound.

REBOUNDING POSITIONS ON SHOTS FROM DIFFERENT ANGLES

Shots from Out Front. These shots taken from different angles, against the 3 out 2 back zone, cause the back-line men to vary their positions in the rebound triangle. When a shot is taken from straight away there is no problem, the rebounders end up in the standard positions as shown in Diagram 181. If a shot is taken from the right side out front, and #3 is pulled up to the foul line extended, as he moves toward the hoop to take a position in the rebound triangle, he will have to observe the positions the other two back-line men have taken. He will have to take the vacant position. Diagram 182 shows the back-line defensive position when a shot is taken out front on the right side. Number 5 moves to the left side of the hoop. Number 4 moves in front of the hoop. Number 3 takes the right side. Numbers 2 and 1 move into the medium rebound positions as shown. The positions are now the same as in Diagram 181. If #4 should have to take the right-hand side position, #3 who is coming back would have to take the middle position in front of the hoop.

Shots from Corner. Shots taken from the corner create two different paths for the back-line men to get to the rebound triangle. The first situation finds the back line underneath and in a straight line as the shot is taken from the corner (Diagram 183). Number 5 moves to the left position, while #4 takes the middle and #3 takes the right side. Numbers 1 and 2 move into the medium positions as shown.

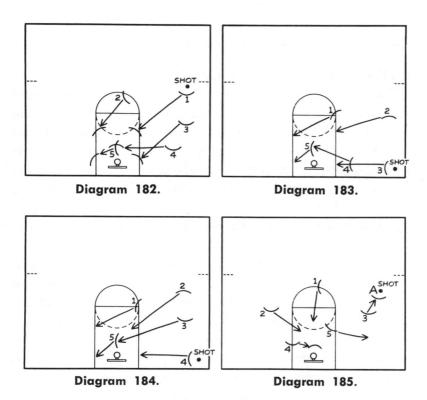

Diagram 182.

Diagram 183.

Diagram 184.

Diagram 185.

When the shooter in the corner is covered by #4, and #3 is up (and on his way back toward the hoop), a problem somewhat similar to the one examined in Diagram 182 is presented. Now, however, the men in the corner and on the side have farther to travel (Diagram 184). Number 3 is on his way back and will take the middle position, number 5 takes the left side and #4 from covering the shooter in the corner will take the right side in the rebound triangle. Numbers 1 and 2 will again assume their medium rebound positions as in Diagram 181.

THREE OUT–TWO BACK REBOUND POSITIONS

When playing the 3 out 2 back zone we try to get the same rebound position with 3 men forming the triangle at the hoop and two men out front guarding the medium rebound area. Diagram 185 depicts the 3 out 2 back zone moving into the standard defensive rebound position.

When the ball is shot from the area of "A" with #3 pulled up to "A," #5 must move over with #4 to the lane in front of the hoop. Number 2 starts his move toward the hoop. If #4 gets pulled halfway to the corner, #1 comes down the middle to the position at the left lane line and dotted line. Number 3 will move in with the shot to the medium-long rebound position. Diagram 186 shows the final position for each player giving us the same rebound setup as in Diagram 181.

When we are using the 2-1-2 sliding zone it is relatively simple to take up our 2 out 3 back rebounding position. We just move the middle man toward the hoop and the front men in and we have the position we desire for rebounding. Diagram 187 shows the moves by the front men and middle man; numbers 4 and 5 just pivot and face the hoop.

Diagram 188 shows the rebounding position after the moves have been completed.

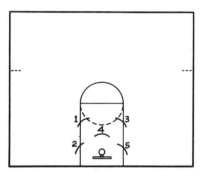 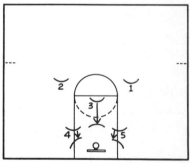

Diagram 186.
Rebound Positions from 3 Out 2 Back Zone (End Up Same as 2 Out 3 Back)

Diagram 187.
Moving from 2-1-2 into 2 Out 3 Back Rebounding Positions

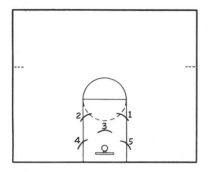

Diagram 188.

TEAM REBOUNDING

It is our opinion that in order to win basketball games you must have a good rebounding team, one which can control the medium-long rebound. This can be done by securing the key defensive positions and taking advantage of floor position. Good floor position on rebounds can compensate for a team's lack of height and strength or the individual skills necessary for controlling rebounds. A team must work hard to learn the defensive rebounding positions employing the triangle of strength near the hoop and maintaining the other two men at the medium rebound position. Make sure your front-line men do not assume their rebound positions too quickly. If they pull out before the rebound is secure, an opening between the front line and back line will appear. This will allow an offensive player to get in between the front and back line and pick up a loose ball or rebound which has fallen into that area. A good rebound position as we have shown will protect the area between front and back line preventing the "cheap" rebound and subsequent shot by the offense.

CONVERSION FROM ZONE DEFENSE TO OFFENSE

The conversion from defense to offense sometimes presents the possibility of a fast break, quick break or a slower advancement of the ball down court where the defense has retreated and awaits the offensive attack. Our main object, offensively, is to get down court before the opponents can set up their defense. In order to accomplish this we must be able to convert from defense to offense as quickly as possible.

Fast Break. The fast break presents the greatest challenge to a defensive team in its efforts to convert to offense. The true fast break is accomplished by an alert defense which both creates and takes advantage of the following opportunities:

1. Interceptions or steals
2. Loose balls and deflections
3. Long rebounds

The nearer the defense is to the mid-court line when it gets the ball the greater the opportunity for the following types of fast-break patterns:

1. One or two men completely alone
2. One-on-one
3. Two-on-one
4. Three-on-two
5. Three-on-three (with trailer)

You must remember that these situations evolved as a result of a steal, interception, or long rebound. The diagrams in this section illustrate the defense retrieving the ball from different situations and positions and then converting into one of the offensive patterns just listed. Diagram 189 shows the interception or steal near mid-court with one man free.

Number 2 intercepts a pass or steals the ball; #1 breaks for the hoop. Number 2 passes to #1 who has an unmolested lay-in shot at the hoop. Numbers 2 and 3 continue in regular fast-break patterns, ready to establish an offensive rebound position. Numbers 4 and 5 move into the offensive half of the court to take their places, one up and one back, in the offensive rebound pattern. (See Diagram 180.)

Diagram 190 shows a loose ball or deflection in the middle of the defense and the fast-break pattern which takes place. The first pass goes from #4 to #2 at the sideline. Number 1 takes the middle position and #3 fills in the third lane on the open side.

Number 2 deflects the ball into the center of the defense. Number 4 retrieves it and passes to #2 on the right sideline, who has already started the fast-break attack. Number 2 takes

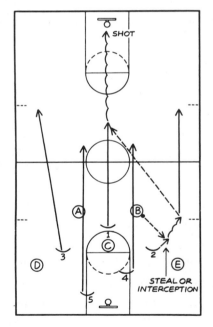

Diagram 189.

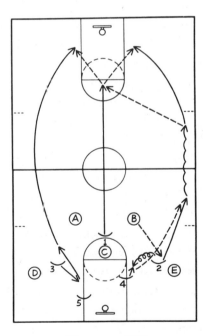

Diagram 190.

the pass and advances by dribbling. Number 1 (in the center lane) will quickly catch up and receive a pass from #2. Number 3 who has started for the defensive hoop now converts and fills the left-hand lane in the fast break. Numbers 4 and 5 again move up to the offensive half of the court and take their offensive rebound positions.

Diagram 191 illustrates the offensive conversion after receiving the long rebound. It is important to note here that if the defensive men are playing their rebound positions properly they will have their backs to their own offensive hoop. Thus, it will take a split second for the players to retrieve the ball, get turned, and head down court. We have found it best for the men retrieving the long rebound to anticipate the turn as they prepare for the rebound. This turn may oftentimes be executed while they are still in the air. Skillful players can turn and clear out the ball to a fast-breaking teammate before they make contact with the floor. We use our clear-out drill to develop this skill. It will be explained in detail later in this chapter.

Diagram 191 shows #2 retrieving the long rebound above the foul line. Number 1 breaks for the left sideline and after receiving the clear-out pass from #2 dribbles down the left in the fast-break attack. Number 2, after passing, takes the middle lane while #5 takes the right-hand lane. Numbers 3 and 4 move into the offensive court and take the up and back rebound positions.

The Quick Break. The quick break is the execution of an offensive play from the fast-break setup which has been stymied. For example, we may get our fast break in position but there may be defensive men guarding us; then we will try a trailer play. (See Diagram 192.) Diagram 192 shows our men in position with the ball at the center position in the fast break but the three men on the break are covered. Here #4 is the trailer and he goes around #1 who has the ball trying to ma-

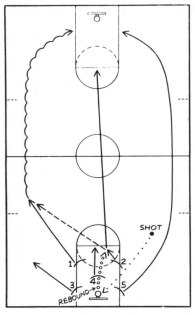

Diagram 191.

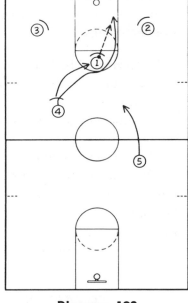

Diagram 192.

neuver his defensive man into the screen set by #1. Then #1 passes to #4 for the shot.

There are an infinite number of screens and plays from this position all involving the one-on-one, two-on-two, and three-on-three, as previously described in Chapter 2.

ADVANCING TO A RETREATED DEFENSE

The opponent's offensive team will often take one shot and then quickly drop back on defense. A team that uses this strategy must rely on accurate shooting and an abundance of rebounding by one or two offensive rebounders. The purpose of retreating quickly is to organize the defensive setup and to be ready for your offensive thrust. This type of defense will frustrate a team which relies on the fast break or a running game. There are two methods of advancing the ball to a retreated defense:

1. Throw the ball in bounds to your best dribbler and let him dribble it to the offensive court.
2. Have your two good ball handlers pass it to one another as they advance the ball up to and over the mid-court line.

This retreated defense should cause no problem for advancing the ball to the offensive court. The retreating play has a tendency to set a slower tempo for the game and, in fact, may be your opponent's objective. Our general counteraction against such a tactic is simply to speed up the game and help get the ball into the offensive half of the court more quickly.

CONVERSION AFTER A GOAL IS SCORED

When a goal is scored the man nearest the hoop reaches up and gets the ball as it comes through the net. We try to gain control of the ball before it hits the floor. The man who retrieves the ball should keep it at shoulder height in passing position in order to pass in bounds quickly. He should step to one side of the hoop or the other clearing the backboard and the rigging which may support the board. If he is right handed and is going to his right he should plant his right foot, the same as a baseball pitcher would, "put his foot on the rubber" and throw with a baseball-type pass to his open teammate going down court. If a right hander retrieves the ball and goes to the left side of the court, he must face the hoop, again plant his right foot, and throw the baseball pass. Once the ball is thrown in and the advance has started down court the offense should look for the fast break, quick break, or a set offense against the retreated or waiting defense.

DETERRING THE FAST BREAK

Oftentimes the team which loses the ball will employ deterring action designed to slow up your conversion from defense to offense. One method of deterring is to have the nearest opponent to the rebounder move right in on him attempting to tie him up for a jump ball or force him to pivot, dribble or even fake before passing. He will harass the man starting the offense by keeping his hands up, hoping to force either the bounce pass, lob pass, or any pass out to the side, rather than allowing the clear-out pass directly down court. In order to facilitate our conversion from defense to offense we work very hard on our clear-out drill.

CLEAR-OUT DRILL

Diagram 193 shows the clear-out drill when a shot is made. In this drill we set up two lines, one at the top of the foul circle facing the hoop. We use three balls, at "A," "B" and "C." The other line is at the right sideline facing down court. The man in line "A" will shoot and, assuming he makes it, will retrieve the ball as it goes through the net. The man "F" at the head of the line will break down court, and "A" will try to give him a pass somewhere between the foul line extended and mid-court. Then "F" will return the ball to the middle line and get on the end of the line. "B" will be the next shooter and "G" will be the next cutter. This procedure should continue until all men have several opportunities from both sides of the court. We have assumed here that the shot was made and the ball was taken out-of-bounds. (See Diagram 193.)

If the shot is missed, it is the shooter's responsibility to retrieve the rebound before it hits the floor, and turn and throw to

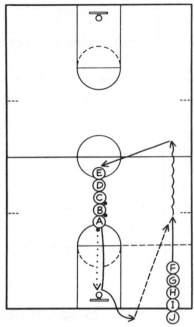

**Diagram 193.   "F" will move to the end of the line behind "E";
"A" will move to the end of the line behind "J."**

the cutter along the sideline using the same technique just explained. Diagram 194 shows the drill from a rebound situation.

After proficiency and skill in this drill have been developed, defensive men may be used first on the shooter, then on the cutter, and finally on both the shooter and cutter. We feel this drill is a necessity for improving the quickness of converting from offense to defense. The combined technique of rebounding and converting from one phase of the game to another (defense to offense or offense to defense) can be improved by the proper execution of this clear-out drill.

CONVERSION FROM OFFENSE TO DEFENSE

In making the conversion from offense to defense it is best

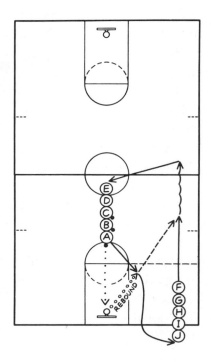

Diagram 194.

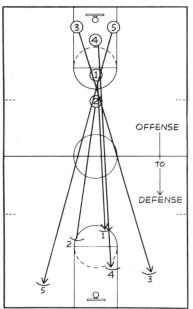

Diagram 195.

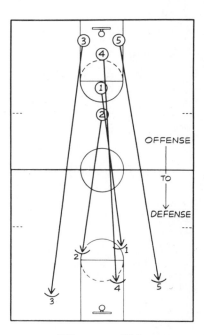

Diagram 196.

to take the shortest and quickest path back to your defensive position. A back-line or front-line man may end up (after an offensive play) on the right side of the court and, in making the conversion from offense to defense, take the long path to a defensive position on the left side of the court at the defensive end. This action not only makes the defensive man run farther, but often causes a collision with a teammate who may decide to cross from the left side of the offensive court to the right side on defense. Diagram 195 illustrates this type of incorrect conversion from offense to defense.

Number 5 coming from the right offensive side to the left defensive side and #3 coming from the left offensive side to the right defensive side not only takes longer but may also cause #3 and #5 to bump into each other as their paths cross, causing a delay which prevents them from getting back on defense in time. This can also happen to the front line unless they are instructed to come straight back. The ideal conversion from offense to defense is shown in Diagram 196.

13

Tips to the Coach

I have explained the construction and development of our Sliding Zone Defense. I feel that it offers a complete defensive system which can meet any challenge presented by the offense. This defensive system breaks down many beliefs that zone defenses are not capable of preventing such tactics as freezing, stalling, screening, and overloading. The Sliding Zone can also be used effectively against the super-star and opponents with superior size and skill. In summary, then, the strengths of the Sliding Zone Defense are listed below:

STRENGTHS OF SLIDING ZONE

1. Eliminates the offensive screening tactic.
2. Provides excellent rebound strength.
3. Discourages offensive driving.
4. Prohibits many close shots.
5. Offers a strong defense for use on small courts.

6. Provides a good formation for starting the fast break.
7. Forces the offense to be deliberate in attacking.
8. Aids big men who do not possess exceptional speed and skill.
9. Adapts readily for half- or full-court pressing.
10. Discourages outside shooting.

SIMPLE TO TEACH

The Sliding Zone is simple to teach if both the coach and his players have a solid background of fundamental basketball. It is a different concept of defensive basketball which deviates from the typical standard defensive game played by the majority of today's basketball teams. The coach who uses a zone of any type for brief intervals will not get the most out of the defense or his players. Usually, tactics of this type, when employed, are used to fool the other team temporarily. Assuming zone positions and "hoping" the offense misses most of its shots may work once in a while, but this does not develop a consistent, aggressive defense. One must sell the defense and convince his players that they are at their best when properly executing these particular defensive fundamentals and slides. The players must believe that the zone tactics will aid them to win games. The coach must understand the basic fundamentals and be adept at conveying these to his players. He must encourage his players to practice them every day under his supervision and guidance.

Half Hour to Teach Basic Defenses. In one-half hour we can teach the basic Sliding Zone (2 out 3 back or 3 out 2 back) to five players who have not been previously exposed to it. During this half hour we can familiarize them with every basic move necessary for success regardless of the zone used. With continued practice and work these defenses can be perfected and developed into a very tenacious unit. For example, we have limited several teams to fewer than eight field goals per game and on two occasions have held teams to four field goals. We are certain that any coach who incorporates the material supplied in this text should be capable of teaching this defense in a very brief amount of time.

Practice Defense Every Day. The defensive slides must be practiced every day in order to achieve proficiency. It takes work—lots of work! We always spent the greatest portion of our practice time on defense. A typical two hour practice session would be as follows:

First Half Hour:	Shoot—15 minutes Running Offensive Plays—15 minutes
Second Half Hour:	Defensive Drills *a*) Front line (one coach supervises) *b*) Back line (another coach supervises)
Third Half Hour:	Stress team defense. Put front and back lines together. Scrimmage full or half court.
Fourth Half Hour:	Work on other phases of game. Fifteen minutes press, 15 minutes offensive drills or any other phase you may wish to work.

In the practice session you must drive your players. Make them hustle and work. Encourage your boys to have pride in their defense by encouraging them when they make a good defensive play. Reward them verbally or by developing a defensive grading system. Give points for blocking shots, stealing the ball, forcing the bad pass, forcing the bad shot, causing a jump ball, and retrieving the rebound. Post the results on your locker-room bulletin board. Explain which defenses are the active ones (presses, full and half court), the "go-get-'em" defenses! Explain the strategies behind every defense. Show them the potential for fast breaking and emphasize the need for a rapid conversion from offense to defense and vice versa.

Developing Teamwork. Developing teamwork is a result of combining the individual front- and back-line drills into a five-man defensive unit. When the parts are inserted into the overall defense, teamwork must be stressed. This includes helping one another by touching-off, using verbal signals and keeping up a steady chatter which is best referred to as "basketball talk." Examples of basketball talk occur when the man covering the offensive man with the ball says "I've got him" or when the front-line man covering the offensive man with the ball yells "I'm up," or "I've got him." The back-line men talk to their front line by such cues as "I'm up," or "You're back." Back-line men should talk among themselves, "I'm back," or "I have the post." This type of chatter is developed during practice sessions. The players may be hesitant to say much at first; however, as they gain confidence in their moves they will also develop confidence in their talking. Consequently, you will discover a fine spirit of teamwork developing as the defensive skills are mastered and the talking becomes an integral part of the defense. The talking must be intelligent, directed toward aiding each man to know what his teammates are doing.

HUMAN ERROR

Human error and fluctuation of performance are important factors for a coach to consider when applying this defense. This factor is brought to light by the statistical records we keep on the players. No one makes all of the shots he attempts. No one passes the ball perfectly every time. No one catches the ball every time it is thrown to him. However, we do know that percentages and records have been improving every season. Improved methods of practice and coaching help make these percentages better. Charts and records have shown the obvious—that shooting percentages are much higher when no one is bothering the shooter. Knowing this factor, we try to bother the offensive player as much as we can, especially when he has the ball. It is imperative for the four defensive men not playing the man with the ball to take positions on the court pre-established with reference to the position of the ball and basket. These positions have been found to be most effective for lowering the statistical percentages of opponents' field goals or limiting the number of shots they may attempt from the good-shooting-percentage areas. This procedure makes the human error factor work in favor of our defense. For example, we fall back and clog the area near the hoop with defensive men and concentrate on those positions which the opponents seem to favor for shooting. We take the positions away from the offense and make them do something they are less accustomed to doing. We try to force them to make long passes, bounce passes, or lob passes; these consume more time than the short, straight pass. This extra time allows our defense to move into position for playing the ball.

FIVE REMINDERS

We have five reminders which we constantly keep telling our players during practice, before a game, and at half time. They are very simple and may well apply to any system of basketball. We have found them to be especially beneficial for aiding our style of play.

They are as follows:

1. Work hard on defense. Do not loaf. When on defense keep your hands up and in defensive position.

2. Get back quickly on defense after we score. (While running back, do not run with your head down looking at the floor or with your back to the ball. Keep your eyes on the ball at all times.)

3. When on defense, talk intelligently so that you can help one another.

4. Be ready and alert on jump balls and out-of-bounds plays. Do not get caught napping and give up an easy goal.

5. When you get the ball take care of it. Do not throw it away or turn it over quickly or easily. When you control the ball you aid your defense.

OTHER TIPS

We have found the following tips to be very helpful in aiding our teaching procedure and the development of player skill.

1. When in practice sessions the ball goes out-of-bounds and rolls away, don't have the players chase it. Assign your managers the task of providing you with another ball and then let the manager chase the out-of-bounds ball.

2. During a game or practice do not allow a player to push, bat, or throw a ball headed for out-of-bounds back into the playing area unless he definitely can get it to a teammate. If he throws it in bounds blindly and it goes to an opponent, a situation of five against four is created since the act of "saving" the ball usually takes the man out of play for several valuable seconds.

3. When teaching the defense make sure the front line learns all of the front-line positions. This axiom holds true for the back line as well.

4. Since boys have a tendency to want to play the same position because of familiarity or security, a possible loss of substitution flexibility may result if the coach does nothing to alter this situation.

The last two suggestions are important reminders to the coach for forcing his players to familiarize themselves with every position.

CONCLUSION

The Sliding Zone Defense incorporates many of the basic techniques of other zone defenses. Its unique features are flexibility and convertibility. Through a process of team movements designed to protect the common scoring areas of the court, the Sliding Zone can employ the specific strengths of several zone formations while eliminating the rigidity which tends to characterize standard zone play. First and foremost, however, the Sliding Zone is an application of fundamental defensive basketball. It makes use of many man-for-man principles. In fact, the defensive man in the Sliding Zone is expected to guard the offensive man with the ball on a man-for-man basis while the other defensive men execute predetermined slides according to the position of the ball relative to the basket. The Sliding Zone presents an opportunity for expression of individual talents and it will blend the individual talents into a collective effort of teamwork.

Factors such as tempo, time remaining, score, calibre and style of opponents, and "foul situation" obviously influence the exact type of Sliding Zone a coach wishes to use. The important point to remember is that the Sliding Zone is capable of adapting to these situations.

The information provided in this text covers approximately forty years of development of the Sliding Zone Defense. It is a sound defensive system which is in its relative infancy (in comparison to other defensive systems). There are opportunities to improve and develop it in order to meet the challenges of the offense and the rule changes which occur. When the Sliding Zone is executed correctly it can defend against any type of offense.

ANSWERS TO QUIZ 1

DEFENSIVE COVERAGE (Answer)

2. 1, 3, 4, 3
3. 1, 3, 4, 3
4. 5, 5
5. 1, 3, 5, 4
6. 1, 4, 5
7. 1, 3, 4, 1
8. 1
9. 3, 2
10. 2, 1, 3
11. 1, 3, 4, 3
12. 1, 3, 4, 3
13. 5, 3

ANSWERS TO QUIZ 2

DEFENSIVE COVERAGE (Answer)

2. 3, 4, 5
3. 2, 5, 2
4. 3, 4, 5, 4
5. 1, 4, 5
6. 2, 5, 4
7. 1, 2, 5, 4
8. 3, 4, 5, 2

ANSWERS TO QUIZ 3

2. 1 5 4

3. 1 5 4 $\frac{2}{5}$
4. 1 5 4 3
5. 1 5 4 1

Index